Central Park

Central

Louise C. Burnham
and George W.W. Packard

Park

A VISIT TO ONE OF THE WORLD'S MOST TREASURED LANDSCAPES

CRESCENT BOOKS
NEW YORK • AVENEL, NEW JERSEY

A FRIEDMAN GROUP BOOK

This 1993 edition published by Crescent Books, distributed by
Outlet Book Company, Inc., a Random House Company,
40 Engelhard Avenue, Avenel, New Jersey 07001.

Copyright © 1993 by Michael Friedman Publishing Group, Inc.

ISBN 0-517-07343-9

CENTRAL PARK
A Visit to One of the World's Most Treasured Landscapes
was prepared and produced by
Michael Friedman Publishing Group, Inc.
15 West 26th Street
New York, New York 10010

Editor: Kelly Matthews
Art Director: Jeff Batzli
Designer: Joseph Rutt
Photography Editor: Anne Price

Typeset by Classic Type, Inc.
Printed and bound in Hong Kong by Leefung-Asco Printers Ltd.

8 7 6 5 4 3 2 1

$\mathcal{D}$ EDICATION

This book is dedicated to the trustees and staff of the Central Park Conservancy and to all who share the Conservancy's commitment to a safe, clean, and beautiful Central Park.

$\mathcal{A}$ CKNOWLEDGMENTS

The authors would like to acknowledge Marianne Cramer, Sherry Dupres, Ruby Isaacs, Dong Kingman, Jr., Harold Levine, Sara Cedar Miller, Betsy Rogers, Laura Starr, and Anne Stetson for their invaluable assistance.

CONTENTS

INTRODUCTION

*I*n the heart of Manhattan, squarely in the midst of the corporate headquarters, theaters, shops, and museums that form the dramatic New York skyline, a park springs up from street level. It runs almost two and a half miles (4 km) long—fifty city blocks—and a half mile (0.8 km) wide, and it serves as a backyard to millions of New Yorkers and as a playground to visitors from all over the globe. In this park you can play baseball or croquet, you can daydream on a lawn, you can take in a live performance of Shakespeare, or you can scan the treetops for a ruby-crowned kinglet, one of the 259 species of birds that frequent the area. You might pass people who are jogging, singing, or cycling. Or you might find yourself sharing your picnic blanket with a stranger while enjoying a symphony performance under the stars.

*B*ethesda Fountain, one of Central Park's most familiar landmarks, enchants visitors from its regal position at the center of Bethesda Terrace.

When Central Park was first designed, the population of New York City was concentrated at the southern end of Manhattan. Today (*right*), the park is a welcoming oasis in the center of the city.

The presence of skyscrapers on the West Side of Manhattan (*opposite*) provides only a modest reminder of the outside world to boaters enjoying a warm autumn day.

Welcome to Central Park, one of the greatest public parks in the world and one of New York City's most celebrated attractions. Since its completion in the middle of the nineteenth century, the park has been an oasis for the residents of New York, providing a mental and physical escape from the frantic pace of the city. In the 1840s, a handful of visionaries understood how important that escape would become. A hundred and fifty years later, we cannot imagine living in New York without it.

Central Park's designers, Frederick Law Olmsted and Calvert Vaux, crafted a work of art on a canvas of natural swampland and bony rock outcrops. Ten million cartloads of stone, earth, and topsoil were moved to or from the area of park; sixty-two miles (100 km) of earthenware drainage pipe was laid; and four million trees, shrubs, and vines were planted. The result is a landscape wholly man-made that looks thoroughly natural.

$\mathcal{V}$isitors of all ages (*above, left*) delight in the various attractions of the park, including the ever-popular sea lion pool at the Central Park Zoo. An outdoor game of chess (*above, right*) under the pergola surrounding the Chess and Checkers House.

The government of New York City, unfortunately, has never provided sufficient resources to care for Central Park. In the 1960s and 1970s, the park nearly died. Today, more than 50,000 individuals, corporations, and foundations have joined together to save Central Park. Founded in 1980, the Central Park Conservancy spearheaded the park's renaissance through an extraordinary public/private partnership with the New York City Department of Parks and Recreation. Thanks to this partnership, Central Park once again offers green lawns, meandering paths, healthy trees, and manicured gardens to a grateful public.

Every year, more than sixteen million people visit Central Park. With so many visitors to accommodate on a regular basis and so many different activities to maintain and regulate, how is it possible to keep everyone who uses and enjoys the park happy? Central Park is a wonderful example of a

community that works together. The Parks Department is careful to designate certain areas for ball-playing and active recreation and preserve other areas for more leisurely pursuits. Permits are drawn up and handed out for the organized use of playing fields, and the Central Park Conservancy coordinates the involvement of parents and school groups for educational purposes. Some of New York City's most highly regarded cultural institutions—the New York Philharmonic, the Metropolitan Opera, the Shakespeare Festival of the Public Theatre—here become active participants in an annual schedule of performing arts. Indeed, on any given day when the sun is shining brightly enough to attract thousands of visitors, Central Park presents New York City at its best, a community peacefully enjoying the out of doors—and each other—side by side.

For those with good eyes and great patience, bird-watching (above, left) is a rewarding pastime in Central Park. Sundays in the park (above, right) are a ritual for thousands of New Yorkers.

A fairy tale carpet of crab apple petals (*right*) line the formal allées of the Conservatory Garden.

A handful of visitors and one lone artist (*opposite*) enjoy the serenity of an early morning at Conservatory Water.

So join us for a stroll through the history and the pathways of Central Park, from its nineteenth-century beginnings in the minds and dreams of poets and politicians to its realization as both an unparalleled work of art and a concourse and common for millions.

CHAPTER ONE

A PARK FOR NEW YORK CITY

A broad sweep of lawn, such as Central Park's Sheep Meadow (*left*), is a precious and much-appreciated commodity for New Yorkers.

THE LAND

In an editorial entitled "A New Park" published in the New York *Evening Post* on July 3, 1844, the poet, naturalist, and newspaper editor William Cullen Bryant called for the establishment of a park for New York City. Bryant picked that date to run the editorial specifically because he knew that with the Independence Day holiday upon them, every New Yorker who could afford to leave town would be escaping to relax in the country. Bryant spoke out against this phenomenon when he wrote, "If the public authorities, who expend so much of our money in laying out the City would do what is in their power, they might give our vast population an extensive pleasure ground for shade and recreation in these sultry afternoons, which we might reach without going out of town."

A year later, Bryant again editorialized in favor of "a range of parks and public gardens along the central part of Manhattan" that would mitigate "the corrupt atmosphere generated in hot and crowded streets." The parks, he declared, would "remain perpetually for the refreshment and recreation of the citizens during the torrid heats of the warm season." He urged, however, that time was running short: "There are yet unoccupied lands on the island which might, I suppose, be procured for the purpose...; but while we are discussing the subject the advancing population of the city is sweeping over them and covering them from our reach."

*W*illiam Cullen Bryant (*above*) was an early champion of a park for Manhattan.

*A*n early map shows the original rectangular plan for the new reservoir before Viele opted for a more naturalistic shape.

New York City's familiar rectangular grid pattern had been developed by the commissioner of streets and roads between 1807 and 1811, but little provision was made for parks. Manhattan Island spans 15,185 acres (6,135 ha), but only 450 acres (182 ha), less than 3 percent, were set aside for parklands in 1811. Even these small parcels of green rapidly succumbed to the pressures of development. By 1853, only 117 acres (47 ha) of parkland remained.

In 1851, New York's population reached 515,000. Well-to-do families fled the congested downtown area and moved north to Twenty-third Street. Thirty-fourth Street formed the city's northern edge. Broadway extended from the Battery northward for more than four miles (6.4 km) to undeveloped land. In 1852, the city extended Fifth Avenue from Thirty-fourth to Forty-fifth Street.

As New York and other American cities grew, the motivations for creating parkland began to multiply. Industry, which had been openly welcomed in the early nineteenth century, soon became part of the urban blight as factories belched black smoke and cluttered cities with ungainly buildings. Fueled by mass immigration, the population explosion brought urban slums, poverty, and street crime to the nation's eastern seaboard. Between 1834 and 1844, there were more than 200 gang wars in New York City alone. As a result, cities developed negative reputations and were viewed as inherently evil.

At the same time, Americans stopped focusing on conquering the wilderness and began to appreciate the grandeur and beauty of their country's landscape. Such painters as Thomas Cole and Frederick Church, who belonged to the first truly American school of painting, the Hudson River School, popularized the scenic Adirondack Mountains and the Hudson River Valley of New York. Ralph Waldo Emerson's writing inspired many of the Hudson River School painters. Written in 1835, one of Emerson's essays, "Nature," suggested that one could seek a mystical union with God in the wilderness. It seems he also inspired Henry

Indeed, by the middle of the nineteenth century New York had become a crowded metropolis. The population, which at the beginning of the century stood at 60,000, had swelled with waves of European immigrants who began arriving in the 1830s. By 1840, there were more than 300,000 New Yorkers. The speed at which the newcomers had to be accommodated left little time for long-range city planning. Instead, the streets, which had been loosely lined with houses, ample yards, and gardens, became more and more densely settled. And what had been rural land above Fourteenth Street was gradually overrun by the northward march of buildings.

David Thoreau, who took Emerson's advice and settled on the shores of Walden Pond.

Whether it was a new appreciation of rural scenery or simply a reaction to the increasing squalor of the city, the urban population began to seek retreats from the cityscape. According to one account, Greenwood Cemetery in Brooklyn drew 60,000 visitors in one season. Built in 1835, Greenwood followed the example of Mt. Auburn Cemetery, which had opened in 1831 outside of Boston, and Laurel Hill Cemetery in Philadelphia. Even though the rural cemeteries were popular, however, many thought that recreation among memorials to the dead was no substitute for the spiritual refreshment available in an uncultivated country setting. As one account described, "Before long, white tombstones and dark lines of hearses took the cheer out of the landscape."

It wasn't long before another call went up to set aside parklands in New York City, this time from Andrew Jackson Downing, whose *Treatise on the Theory and Practice of Landscape Gardening* had established him as America's first professional landscape architect. Taking up Bryant's theme in his publication, *The Horticulturist*, Downing appealed to national vanity. Writing from London in August 1850, Downing noted, "I will merely say…that every American who visits London, whether for the first or fiftieth time, feels mortified that no city in the United States has a public *park* —here so justly considered both the highest luxury and necessity in a great city. What are called parks in New York are not even apologies for the thing; they are only squares or paddocks." Agreeing with Downing, the journalist and politician Horace Greeley wrote a year later, "The parks, squares and public gardens of London beat us clear out of sight."

In truth, the parks movement begun by Bryant and Downing in the United States was only twenty years behind a similar movement in England. There had long been parks in England, but they were hunting grounds and gardens owned by the aristocracy. As the Industrial Revolution prompted the growth of towns and cities, some of these pri-

*A*ndrew Jackson Downing was America's first landscape architect.

vate lands were opened to the public. But it wasn't until 1833 that the British Parliament considered having the government establish parks itself. In that year, Parliament asked a select committee "to consider the best means of securing open spaces in the vicinity of populous Towns as Public Walks and Places of Exercise, calculated to promote the Health and Comfort of the Inhabitants." Having assessed the new urbanization of the population, the committee reported their concern that the population of large towns was increasing, that the working classes were engaged primarily in mechanical production, and that buildings were

A photo taken in 1857 shows how the land was flooded to create the Central Park Lake. The shanties and pigsties in the background would be on present-day Eighth Avenue.

consuming all available open space. They suggested that a provision be made for space to support "the comfort, health and content of the classes in question."

The concerns outlined by Parliament's select committee were passionately embraced by Bryant and Downing. The two editors so successfully persuaded New Yorkers of the need for a park that both mayoral candidates for the 1850 election prominently featured a park for New York in their campaign platforms. The victor, Ambrose C. Kingsland, sent a directive to the common council in 1851 that called for the creation of a park:

Such a park, well laid out, would become the favorite resort of all the classes. There are thousands who pass the day of rest among the idle and dissolute, in porter-

houses, or in places more objectionable, who would rejoice in being enabled to breathe the pure air in such a place, while the ride and drive through its avenues, free from the noise, dust and confusion inseparable from all thoroughfares, would hold out strong inducements for the affluent to make it a place of resort....

The establishment of such a park would prove a lasting monument to the wisdom, sagacity and forethought of its founders, and would secure the gratitude of thousands yet unborn, for the blessing of pure air, and the opportunity for innocent, healthful enjoyment.

The council agreed and recommended the purchase of an area known as Jones Wood, a site that Bryant had first recommended in 1844. The Wood ran along the shore of the East River between Sixty-eighth and Seventy-seventh Streets and was, according to Bryant, "a tract of beautiful woodland, thickly covered with old trees, intermingled with a variety of shrubs." In July 1851, New York's state legislature authorized the purchase of the site.

The Jones Wood site totaled only 160 acres (65 ha), however, and both Downing and Bryant immediately called for a larger site to be selected. In August 1851, Downing wrote:

Five hundred acres is the smallest area that should be reserved.... In that area there would be space enough to have broad reaches of park and pleasure-grounds, with a real feeling of the breadth and beauty of green fields, the perfume and freshness of nature.... In such a park, the citizens who would take excursions in carriages, or on horseback, could have the substantial delights of country roads and country scenery, and forget for a time the rattle of the pavements and the glare of brick walls. Pedestrians would find quiet and secluded walks when they wished to be solitary, and broad alleys filled with thousands of happy faces, when they would be gay. The

thoughtful denizen of the town would go out there in the morning to hold converse with the whispering trees, and the wearied tradesman in the evening, to enjoy an hour of happiness by mingling in the open spaces with "all the world."

A combination of factors brought about the selection of a site that was larger, more central, and at the time, not highly desired by private developers. "The Central Park," as it was first called, extended from Fifty-ninth Street to One Hundred and Sixth Street, but a subsequent purchase of sixteen acres (6.5 ha) of low-lying land north of the rocky cliffs at One Hundred and Sixth Street brought the northern border to One Hundred and Tenth Street and the site's total acreage to 840 (339 ha). Between 1853 and 1856, the commissioners of assessment took the land, paying $5,069,693 to 7,500 owners and assessing those who owned property that would surround the park a surtax totaling $1,657,590.

An ordinance adopted by the common council on May 19, 1856, named the mayor and the street commissioner as commissioners of the project. A number of New York's most well-regarded citizens were asked to join them, including Washington Irving, who was elected president at the board's first meeting. A year later, fearing that the construction of Central Park would be hampered by partisan politics, the state legislature appointed an independent group of eleven commissioners who first met on April 30, 1857.

The first of the two boards appointed Egbert Viele to the position of chief engineer. Viele had graduated from West Point in 1847 and, after serving with the army in Mexico, had become a civil engineer. Viele had worked on plans for the park on speculation and was gratified that in the first report of the commissioners his plan was published with the note "Adopted, June 3, 1856." With the governance of the project established and with a design in hand, the common council appropriated $100,000 for the development of the park, and work to clear the land commenced.

*F*rederick Law Olmsted's career as the nineteenth century's most prolific landscape architect began with Central Park.

THE DESIGNERS

Frederick Law Olmsted had not participated in the public debate for Central Park. The eldest son of a wealthy Hartford merchant, Olmsted grew up in comfort, but without any particular ambition. His father, John Olmsted, had had little formal education, but instilled in his son a deep love of rural scenery. Olmsted later wrote that before he was twelve, he had ridden "over the most charming roads of the Connecticut Valley and its confluents, through the White Hills and along most of the New England coast from the Kennebeck to the Naugatuck....I had also traveled much with my father and mother by stagecoach, canal and steamboat, visiting West Point, Trenton Falls, Niagara, Quebec, and Lake George."

Like his father, Olmsted's formal education was scant. He boarded with various clergymen; three sent him to day school and the fourth tutored him in preparation for Yale College. Poor eyesight prevented him from matriculating at Yale, but he spent one semester at the school visiting his younger brother.

In 1840, at the age of eighteen, Olmsted moved to New York City and took a job at a dry-goods importing firm. For the next sixteen years, always restless and full of enthusiasm for the next venture, he tried one career after another, constantly relying on his father for financing. The job at the importing firm lasted for a little more than a year, at which point Olmsted signed on for a yearlong trip to China. He returned pale, underweight, and sick with scurvy in 1843.

Olmsted's next endeavor was farming. After an apprenticeship with a farmer in upstate New York, Olmsted persuaded his father to buy him a small farm in Sachem's Head, Connecticut. Two years later, he sold the land and purchased a larger farm on Staten Island. Neither was a financial success, but Olmsted's proximity to New York City gave him the opportunity to form friendships with men who shared his interest in scientific farming, including Andrew Jackson Downing.

When his brother John arranged a trip to England with a college friend two years later, however, Olmsted, discouraged by the rigors of farm life, asked his father if he could go as well. Olmsted chronicled the trip in a small volume, and when *Walks and Talks of an American Farmer in England* was first published in 1852, it launched his writing career. The book was soon followed by articles in Downing's *Horticulturist* and a commission by the New York *Daily Times* to report on the social conditions in the antebellum South. His letters and resultant two-volume work, *The Cotton Kingdom*, remain some of the most enduring portraits of the U.S. plantation culture.

This eclectic set of experiences would serve Olmsted surprisingly well in his future role as architect of Central Park. His study of scientific farming and his tour of England, which included a thorough inspection of the country's parks, gave him a solid grounding in both botany and landscape design. His travels in the South also influenced his work on the park. Olmsted's dismay at the condition of life in the southern countryside and on the western frontier in Texas made him a strong supporter of such institutions as museums, libraries, and parks, because of their ability to refine and disseminate cultural values.

It was a chance meeting in 1857 that set Olmsted on the path to a lifelong career in landscape architecture and urban planning. At a seaside inn in Morris Cove, Connecticut, while immersed in completing his book on Texas, *Journey in the Back Country*, Olmsted happened to meet Charles Wyllis Elliott, one of the eleven Central Park commissioners. When Olmsted inquired about the park project, Elliott told him that the commission was in search of a superintendent who would be responsible for overseeing the building of the park. The idea so intrigued Olmsted that he left for New York that night to begin his campaign for the job. In his favor, Olmsted's literary career had acquainted him with the New York elite; Horace Greeley, William Cullen Bryant, August Belmont, Asa Gray, and Washington Irving all endorsed his candidacy. He was also a nonpolitical Republican who fitted the commission's need for political balance, having already elected a Democratic president and treasurer. On the other hand, Olmsted had a reputation as a man of letters, not as a "practical man" who could oversee thousands of workers. Nevertheless, his personal supporters triumphed, and

*A*n 1860 view of the Ramble looking west toward the Park Drive as it crosses Balcony Bridge.

Olmsted was elected superintendent in September 1857, at an annual salary of $1,500.

Despite his political victory, Olmsted's literary and impractical image would haunt him as he assumed his new role. On his first day of work, Olmsted arrived at the park site wearing formal clothes and reported to his new boss, Egbert Viele. Viele, rather unimpressed by the man who stood before him, sent him off on a tour of the site with a Mr.

*S*panning the western arm of the Lake was Oak Bridge (*left*), a decorative structure of milled white oak and open cast iron panels.

*W*hen the park was built, New York's Upper East Side was a rural area (*above*) dotted with squatters' shacks.

Hawkin, who appeared coatless and wearing big, muddy boots. The heat of the sunny day and the swampy landscape soon made Olmsted regret his sartorial selection. The laborers were amused at the sight of the well-dressed literary man who was to be their boss. It was Olmsted, however, who was to have the last laugh. Initially, Olmsted wrote of the laborers, who had been hired more for their political connections than for their skills or brawn, that "the idea that I might expect a good day's work from them for each day's due-bill was thought a good joke." By January, however, he wrote to his father, "I have got the park into a capital discipline, a perfect system, working like a machine—1,000 men now at work." What no one had known, least of all Olmsted, was that despite a checkered early career, Olmsted possessed a remarkable talent for administration.

His relationship with Viele, however, never improved. Viele was upset that although the first board of commissioners had adopted his plan for Central Park, the second board, which was elected in April 1857, decided to set the plan aside and hold a national competition for the park's design. A young British architect named Calvert Vaux asked Olmsted to join him in entering the contest, but Olmsted was concerned that Viele would disapprove. When Olmsted finally broached the subject, Viele scornfully replied that it was a matter of complete indifference to him.

Calvert Vaux (the x is pronounced) had met Andrew Jackson Downing at the Architectural Association of London in 1850, and impressed by Vaux's work, Downing had invited him to travel to the United States and become his assistant. Vaux agreed and settled in Newburgh-on-Hudson, where Downing lived. Their brief partnership was a productive one; they collaborated on many private residences and together conceived the plan for the mall in Washington, D.C. Their partnership ended abruptly and tragically when a riverboat accident took Downing's life in 1852. Had he lived, there is little doubt that Downing himself would have designed Central Park.

The site selected for the park posed an enormous challenge to the two young designers. Shortly after Olmsted began work as superintendent, he wrote to his brother, "I had not been aware that the Park was such a very nasty place. In fact, the low grounds were steeped in the overflow of mush of pigsties, slaughterhouses and bone-boiling works, and the stench was sickening." In another letter, he described the area as "a pestilential spot, where rank vegetation and miasmatic odors taint every breath of air." There were few trees worthy to grace the new park; most of the ground was swamp, pools of stagnant water, or jagged rock outcrops.

A contemporary park commissioner described the southern portion as "already a part of [New York's] straggling suburbs, a suburb more filthy, squalid and disgusting can hardly be imagined." The residents of Seneca Village, a collection of squatters' shacks located west of the Old Croton Reservoir (now the Great Lawn) resisted their eviction. The police succeeded in emptying the area after park workers had tried to no avail. Left behind were the park's first pests, an infestation of goats, which as late as 1858 prompted the board of commissioners to urge the common council to amend their ordinance for impounding stray animals to include goats. "The trees have already suffered much from these animals; they are very numerous in the neighborhood of the Park."

The combination of Vaux's professional experience and Olmsted's farm work, travels abroad, and intimate knowledge of the park site enabled the designers to turn this "pestilential swamp" into a work of art. The two spent long hours after work during the week and all day on Sundays hammering out the details of their design. When they were working on the final drawings, according to a later account by Vaux's son Downing, "there was a great deal of grass to be put in by the usual small dots and dashes, and it became the friendly thing for callers to help on the work by joining and 'adding some grass to Central Park.'" Olmsted and Vaux signed their plan "Greensward," and submitted it on April 1, 1858. A month later, Greensward was declared the winner.

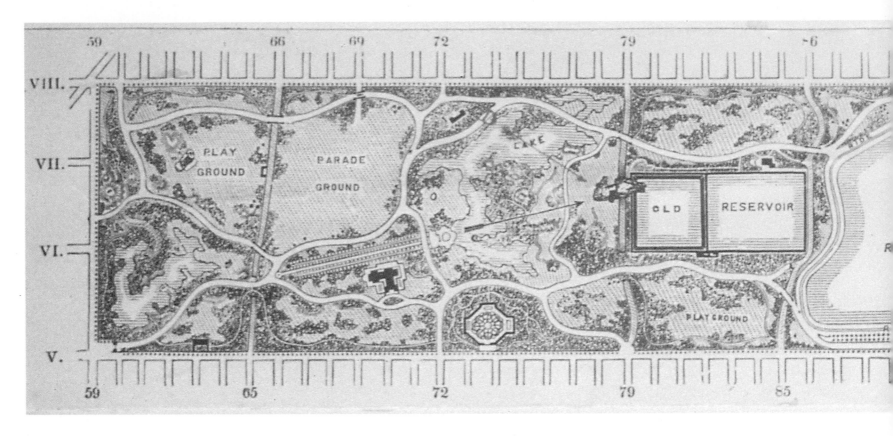

THE PLAN

Well after the Greensward Plan won the competition, Olmsted described the park as "a single work of art, and as such subject to the primary law of every work of art, namely, that it shall be framed upon a single noble motive, to which the design of all its parts, in some more or less subtle way, shall be confluent and helpful." That motive, as Bryant, Downing, and others had described, was the furnishing of a large rural landscape at the center of what was already the largest city in the country. Olmsted and Vaux's goal was to create a rural retreat that would be "remedial of the influences of urban conditions...[with] pure and wholesome air ...[and] an antithesis of objects of vision to those of the streets and houses which should act remedially by impressions on the mind and suggestions to the spirit."

The motive went further. Not only would the park serve as a rural oasis, but it would become a symbol of American democracy. In a letter published in 1848, Andrew Jackson Downing described the public garden of Frankfurt, Germany, which "is open to every man, woman and child in the city....50,000 souls have the right to enter and enjoy these beautiful grounds; and yet, though they are most thoroughly enjoyed, you will no more see a bed trampled upon, or a tree injured, than in your own private garden here at home.... There is truly a democracy in that, worth imitating in our more professedly democratic country." Olmsted's vision for Central Park was to create a similarly democratic space.

Democracy in Downing's, and later Olmsted's, words meant a park created and maintained by the public for its own health and contentment. Unlike the royal parks of England, Central Park was created by a democratic government at the request of its constituents. The first such park in England was built at Birkenhead, outside of Liverpool. In

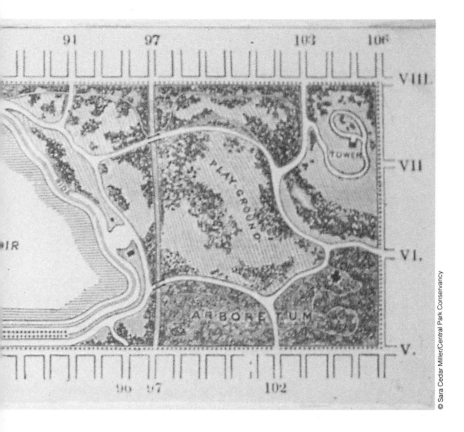

Olmsted and Vaux illustrated their competition entry with a number of renderings of various views. This woodcut (*left*), a schematic plan outlining their design, appeared throughout the presentation to locate the sketches.

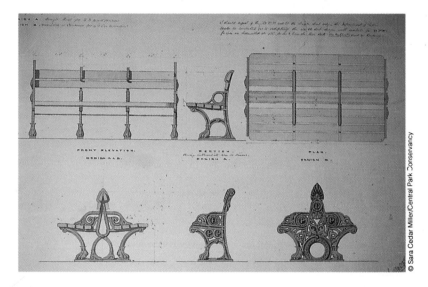

Jacob Wrey Mould designed a series of benches (*above*) for Central Park in the 1870s.

Walks and Talks of an American Farmer in London, Olmsted described his visit to Birkenhead, where he was accosted by a baker who begged him to visit "our park" before he left. Olmsted was impressed by what he saw. "I was ready to admit that in democratic America there was nothing to be thought of as comparable to this people's garden."

More impressive to Olmsted than the landscape itself was the democratic ideal it expressed. "All of this magnificent pleasure-ground is entirely, unreservedly, and for ever the people's own. The poorest British peasant is as free to enjoy it in all its parts as the British queen. More than that, the baker of Birkenhead has the pride of an OWNER in it…. Is it not a good thing?"

Andrew Jackson Downing had predicted in 1849 that this kind of democratic development would "largely civilize and refine the national character, foster the love of rural beauty, and increase the knowledge of, and taste for, rare and beauti-

ELEVATION.

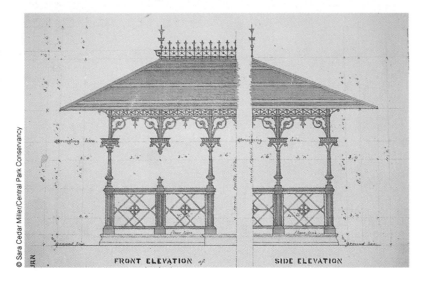

FRONT ELEVATION of   SIDE ELEVATION

*M*ould prepared this study for
Gapstow Bridge (*top*) in 1874; the bridge was replaced with a sturdier
stone arch before the turn of the century. The Ladies Pavilion
(*above*), now on the western bank of the Lake, once served as a bus
shelter at Columbus Circle, outside the southwest corner of the park.

ful plants." He added, "The true policy of republics is to foster the taste for public libraries, parks and gardens which *all* may enjoy." Olmsted agreed: "[Central Park] is of great importance as the first real park made in this country—a democratic development of the highest significance and on the success of which…much of the progress of art and esthetic culture in the country is dependent."

The design of the Greensward Plan may also be labeled democratic. Olmsted and Vaux followed the Romantic, naturalistic landscape tradition that had begun in the eighteenth century when the English broke away from the formal geometric garden perfected by the French under the architect Le Notre, who laid out the gardens at Versailles. To the English, the geometry symbolized French authoritarian rule and the desire to control nature. The English were more interested in nature's ability to inspire the senses, a quality to which Romantic poets such as Wordsworth paid tribute. In the middle of the eighteenth century, a landscape architect by the name of Lancelot "Capability" Brown swept away the formal gardens and allées of many English estates and replaced them with naturalistic scenes. The landscapes of these estates were called "parks," although they were used by their owners primarily for hunting game. Brown felt strongly that the park landscape should come straight up to the door of the house, unmediated by a garden, to provide the building with a more architectural context.

Brown's landscape conveyed a sense of gentle serenity that can be classified as pastoral. An amateur contemporary of Brown, Sir Uvedale Price, admired Brown's park landscapes, where the sweep of gently undulating green lawn was accentuated by clumps of trees and a broad river winding in and out of view. On the whole, however, Price thought Brown's style too gentle and too serene. His landscapes lacked roughness, sudden variation, and irregularity of form. These qualities comprised the picturesque landscape, a term that originally referred to the works of landscape artists such as Claude Lorrain and Nicolas Poussin. Price's picturesque was savage and wild, producing melancholy rather than serenity. Sir Humphrey Repton, who succeeded Brown as the leader of the English Landscape School, established a compromise position that blended the pastoral scene of Brown's private parks with Price's appreciation for the picturesque.

Andrew Jackson Downing brought the aesthetic tradition of the English Landscape School to the estates he designed along the Hudson River. This aesthetic he also passed on to Vaux who, having spent much of his life in the English countryside and in London's parks, was well steeped in the naturalistic style, as was Olmsted after his tour of Great Britain.

The Greensward Plan exhibited both the sweeping meadows of the pastoral landscape and the rocky irregularity of the picturesque. The variety of landforms at the original park site precluded the creation of an entirely pastoral landscape. Tranquil scenes would comprise much of the park, and the remaining land would, as the designers wrote, "form passages of scenery contrasting in depth of obscurity and picturesque character of detail with the softness and simplicity of the open landscape." The creation of Central Park established the vocabulary and design values of the English Landscape School as the model for urban parks across North America, many of which would be designed by Olmsted himself.

But the Greensward Plan was more than a masterpiece of landscape art. It was also a prophetic piece of urban planning. In the written description that accompanied their winning design, Olmsted and Vaux wrote, "Up to this time, in planning public works for the city of New York, in no instance has adequate allowance been made for its increasing population and business....A wise forecast of the future gave the proposed park the name of Central....Only twenty years ago Union Square was 'out of town'; twenty years hence, the town will have enclosed the Central Park."

The design competition had called for four roads that would bear traffic across the park. Olmsted and Vaux, probably drawing on their knowledge of an underpass at the

This wisteria arbor with welcoming rustic benches was located near what is now the Heckscher Ballfields.

Regents Park Zoo in London, envisioned sunken transverse roads spanned by bridges. The four roads, at Sixty-fifth, Seventy-ninth, Eighty-sixth, and Ninety-sixth Streets, would keep the cross-park traffic from interrupting the visitor's rural park experience. Not only would the walled roads keep the sights and sounds of traffic out of the park, they would also allow the park to close at night while the transverses remained open.

The transverse roads were but one example of the designers' ingenuity. Equally imaginative was the park's circulation system that separated foot, carriage, and equestrian traffic into seventy miles (112 km) of paths that rarely intersected. A century earlier, Capability Brown had introduced traffic separation on a private estate, but never before had the idea been executed on such a grand scale. Thirty-eight bridges, each designed by Vaux, led pedestrians beneath the carriage traffic or above the Bridle Trail.

The carriage road, or park drive, traces an oval around the perimeter of the park. Traffic proceeds in a counterclockwise direction: northward along the east drive and southward on the west drive, which, planted thickly with evergreens, was originally termed the "winter drive." Frequent curves were designed to treat drivers and passengers to a constantly changing succession of views and, more practically, to eliminate straightaways that might prompt "trotting matches" between carriages.

*W*orkers blasted a tunnel beneath Vista Rock when they built the sunken transverse road across Seventy-ninth Street. The fire tower atop the rock is on the site of the Belvedere, built in 1871.

$\mathscr{A}$ couple enjoys a quiet moment by the Lake. The urns filled with flowers on Bow Bridge disappeared by 1900.

One of the challenges of the park site was the new reservoir, which practically split the park in two. Olmsted and Vaux wrote about the two halves as the upper and lower parks and set the dividing line at the Eighty-sixth Street transverse road. About the upper park, they wrote: "The horizon lines…are bold and sweeping and the slopes have great breadth….As this character is the highest ideal that can be aimed at for a park…and as it is in most decided contrast to the confined and formal lines of the city it is desirable to interfere with it…as little as possible. Formal planting and architectural effects, unless on a very grand scale, must be avoided."

"The lower park," they wrote, "is more heterogeneous in character and will require a much more varied treatment." The lower park therefore became the site of nearly all of the park's buildings, its formal promenade, and the children's district. The eastern border of the lower park allowed for the development of the pastoral rolling meadows of the Dene

and Cedar Hill, but the western border was rocky and due for more picturesque treatment.

Throughout the design, Olmsted and Vaux aimed to convey a sense of spaciousness. One tactic was to obscure the buildings around the park's perimeter by planting a row of trees along Fifth Avenue and Eighth Avenue (now Central Park West) and along Fifty-ninth and One Hundred and Tenth Streets. Within the park, curving pathways gave visitors a succession of views as they walked or rode along. The only exception was the promenade, now called the Mall, which Olmsted and Vaux considered "an essential feature of a metropolitan park." This they envisioned as the "grand promenade" for park visitors with social objectives. Lined by a quadruple row of elm trees, the promenade led visitors to the park's grandest architectural feature, Bethesda Terrace, on the shore of the Lake. The Terrace lay below the view of the promenader, who looked instead across the Lake to the woodland called the Ramble, crowned by a miniature castle,

It was believed that mature elm trees would survive transplanting, which was one reason they were chosen to line the Mall. But the trees that were originally planted all died, and these saplings took their place in 1863.

the Belvedere. Both the size of the Castle and the planting design of the trees in the Ramble—darker trees on the perimeter and lighter trees in the interior—added depth to the view and made the Castle look farther away.

Swamps and small streams dotted the original park site, but Olmsted and Vaux felt that sheets of water were more interesting than "mere rivulets." They therefore developed four large lakes: the Pond at Fifty-ninth Street, the Lake at Seventy-second, the Pool at West One Hundred and Second, and the Harlem Meer at One Hundred and Tenth. Other water was drained into a system of pipes more than ninety-five miles (152 km) long. With the exception of the Meer, all of the lakes were fed by the city water supply.

An Austrian named Ignaz Pilat helped translate Olmsted and Vaux's vision for the park into a detailed planting scheme. Neither of the park's designers possessed a knowledge of plants sufficient for the task, though Olmsted's farming career had provided basic training. Pilat had studied at the botanical gardens of the University of Vienna and at the Imperial Botanical Gardens at Schonbrunn. Political difficulties brought Pilat to America in 1848. After laying out the grounds of a number of estates in Georgia and then returning briefly to Vienna as the director of the botanical gardens, Pilat was asked in 1857 to join the park project. He agreed and remained dedicated to Central Park until his death in 1870.

Pilat's contribution to the park's development cannot be overstated. The Greensward Plan, Olmsted and Vaux cautioned, was merely the starting point for the design of the park. Pilat helped bring the designers' vision to life as he directed the planting of more than four million trees, shrubs, and vines. The selection and placement of the trees in particular defined the park's physical spaces and gave them their aesthetic character. Only by working together could Pilat, Olmsted, and Vaux translate the vision of the Greensward Plan into a fully realized work of art.

*T*he grand double staircase at
Bethesda Terrace features intricate sandstone carvings designed by
Jacob Wrey Mould.

CHAPTER TWO

FIGHTING FOR
THE PARK

It took twenty years after the approval of the Greensward Plan to complete Central Park. Hampered by an endless series of political battles, Olmsted, who became architect-in-chief in November 1858, and Vaux, who served as assistant to the architect-in-chief (Viele's position was abolished), officially resigned many times. A good portion of the problems stemmed from Tammany Hall, the democratic machine that dominated New York politics from 1850 until 1933. But more significantly, the very nature of the park as a public institution dictated that the construction, management, and later reconstruction would be a highly political process. The people of New York City, like the baker of Birkenhead, were proud of their park, and because they considered themselves part-owners, they were concerned about its progress.

SPOILERS AND DEFENDERS

From the beginning, Olmsted and Vaux had an exceedingly difficult relationship with the park's controller, Andrew Haswell Green. Not connected with the Tammany crowd who fought for control of the park project's thousands of jobs to reward their faithful, Green was an honest, dedicated, and diligent guardian of New York's finances. But he was, perhaps, conscientious to a fault. Despite Olmsted's remarkable ability and talent in organizing and motivating a large workforce, Green's insistence on his accounting for every penny not only irritated Olmsted but also occasionally

At times, the city seems like the park's inquisitive neighbor, looking over a border of trees as if to ask permission to come out and play.

impeded progress and on more than one occasion led to the architect-in-chief's resignation. These disagreements aside, Green admired Olmsted and Vaux's vision and at times was their most ardent supporter. As work on the park moved forward, however, it became clear that Green's fastidious accounting practices were but a minor nuisance when compared with far greater threats to the park, the first of which came at the height of the Tweed Ring scandal.

William Marcy Tweed was the first boss of Tammany Hall, where he earned his nickname, Boss Tweed. Until a county bookkeeper named Matthew O'Rourke exposed the fraud, Tweed used his political influence to abscond with more than two hundred million dollars in public funds. He also introduced a new city charter in 1870, which, among other things, abolished the state-appointed board of commissioners of Central Park and put control of the park back in city hands. Tammany installed four loyal henchmen on the new five-man commission. Green remained on the board but for once was powerless to control the park project.

The Tammany commissioners did not accept Olmsted and Vaux's vision for the park and quickly set about implementing their own. Picturesque plantings were "cleaned up" and

trees were removed or else trimmed of their lower branches to secure "circulation of air," to "open beautiful views," and to clear the park of "tangled weeds." The commissioners also drew up plans for buildings that, fortunately, were never built. O'Rourke's whistle-blowing brought on the end of the Tweed Ring, and in November 1871, a new board of commissioners was appointed.

The Tweed scandal, however, did little to break the power of Tammany Hall. Three years later, a new Tammany administration formed a park board with two Tammany Democrats and two Republicans. Little progress could be made under their stalemated supervision, and in 1877, Olmsted resigned for the last time. Over fifty prominent citizens joined together to protest Olmsted's departure, but his decision was final. In a pamphlet, *The Spoils of the Park, With a Few Leaves from the Deep-Laiden Books of "A Wholly Impractical Man,"* Olmsted chronicled the scenes of petty municipal politics that had finally driven him to resign for good.

Calvert Vaux maintained his ties to the park project even after Olmsted's departure, serving as superintending architect to the department of public parks from 1881 to 1882 and

A turn-of-the-century gondola ride (*opposite, bottom*) was only as private as the nearest bank of curious onlookers. The gondola was donated by John A.C. Gray, one of the original commissioners of Central Park. Horse-drawn carriages (*opposite, top*) were the primary mode of transportation when the park was opened.

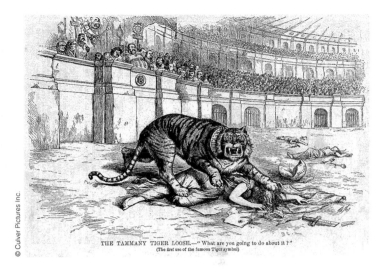

© Culver Pictures Inc.

THE TAMMANY TIGER LOOSE.—"What are you going to do about it?"
(The first use of the famous Tiger symbol)

The power of the Tammany Hall democratic machine was perceived to be voracious (*left*), as a contemporary cartoon illustrated.

as landscape architect from 1888 until his death in 1895. Vaux provided Central Park with one of its most ardent defenders when he hired Samuel Parsons to become superintendent of planting in 1882. Parsons' father, a distinguished horticulturist of the time, owned a nursery in Flushing, New York, and supplied many of Central Park's original trees and shrubs. His *The Rose: Its History, Poetry, Culture and Classification* remains a classic in its field.

Parsons would devote nearly thirty years to Central Park. Although Vaux continued the practice of resigning as a means of fighting threats to the park's integrity, Parsons' tenure was interrupted only once. Parsons resigned during the interlude when Egbert Viele was appointed to the board of commissioners in 1883 and became its president for six months in 1884. Viele, still bitter from having been bested in the design competition, fought every plan advanced by Parsons and Vaux. Fortunately, the mayoral election of 1884 brought William R. Grace to power and with him came a new park board. Grace was Parsons' ally, and on May 25, 1885, he installed Parsons as superintendent of Central Park and the other parks of Manhattan and the Bronx.

At this point, Central Park was nearly complete. Parsons became the first administrator to face the challenge of maintaining the park with a minimal budget and, consequently, a workforce that was too small for the job. Parsons was as gifted an administrator as he was a plants man, but the decline of Central Park nevertheless began during his tenure.

Parsons struggled mightily to keep Olmsted and Vaux's vision alive. Because the park's 840 acres (339 ha) were in the center of Manhattan, it was vulnerable to encroachments of every conceivable kind, particularly after the state legislature voted to build the Metropolitan Museum of Art inside the park wall at East Eighty-second Street in 1868. With such a precedent, Olmsted, Vaux, and Parsons had to fight hard to keep structures and statuary out of the park. Parsons' victories included politely steering the family of Ulysses S. Grant to select a site for Grant's tomb outside of Central Park even though they had been offered the choice of a site anywhere in the city. Parsons could also take credit for ensuring that the William Tecumseh Sherman statue was erected at Grand Army Plaza rather than at the southern end of the Mall.

𝒯he park drive winds past the Metropolitan Museum, the obelisk, and in the distance, the old reservoir.

In his memoirs, Parsons described the cause of yet another fight: a proposal that came at a time when fast driving was at the height of fashion. "With the usual tendency of classes to demand special privilege in parks which were made for the people, it was suggested that a race track be built on the west boundary of Central Park." Construction of the speedway actually commenced and was halted only when the uproar in the press caused Tammany Hall concern. The working classes were none too pleased by the project, and Tammany did not want to lose their vote. In a dramatic about-face, construction ceased, and the speedway was eventually built on the shore of the Harlem River between One Hundred and Fifty-sixth and Two Hundred and Second Streets. "Eternal vigilance and plenty of backbone and tact," Parsons wrote, "are evidently the price of the retention of a park; that is, a park in the true sense of the word."

Parsons resigned in 1911 as the result of a dispute with the board of commissioners. Central Park historian Henry Hope Reed calls Parsons' departure the end of the "Greensward Dynasty." Not until the late 1970s would the park again be managed by someone sympathetic to Olmsted and Vaux's belief that in rural scenery urban dwellers find the most restorative antidote to the press of crowds and concrete.

THE CHANGING LANDSCAPE

The last years of Parsons' tenure marked the beginning of a new reform movement that would leave an indelible mark on the park. Whereas Bryant, Downing, Olmsted, and Vaux had all argued that fresh air and the civilizing influence of beautiful rural scenery would improve the lot of the city's underprivileged, the new reformers took a more active role. Their energy and commitment built settlement houses, public baths, and playgrounds in the poorest areas of the city. And in Central Park, the reformers saw a great resource for programmed recreation.

At the turn of the century, Central Park hosted many sporting events: skating, lawn tennis, baseball, basketball,

Larger threats loomed. One of Theodore Roosevelt's uncles proposed that the city raise funds by selling off the southern border of the park in building lots and purchasing cheaper land for the park north of One Hundred and Tenth Street. Later, the board of commissioners offered the North Meadow as a suitable site for the World's Fair of 1893. Vaux, Parsons, and Andrew Green stood firm, as did the state Republican boss, Thomas Platt. Civic pride tugged hard, however, and the mayor was enthusiastic. One park commissioner suggested that all of the trees in and around the North Meadow be temporarily transplanted. Another suggested that a floor could be built over the new reservoir and the fair should be held on top of it. Fortunately, Chicago had lined up more votes in Congress for their city to be the site than had New York, and Central Park was spared.

football, croquet, and more. In 1915, more than 20,000 tennis permits were issued. Temporary courts were set up on the Sheep Meadow, and clay courts were installed on the South Meadow, where they remain today. In the 1920s, the reformers organized a barrage of contests: canoe regattas and swimming meets on the lake, miniature airplane and sailboat races, roller-skating and ice-skating derbies, tennis tournaments and even marble-shooting contests. Some of these activities did little harm to the park. But the lawn sports exacted a heavy toll on the park's turf.

Debate over the use of the lawns had raged since the park's earliest days. Olmsted and Vaux first identified the problem in 1865: "It seems difficult for [ballplayers] to realize that the large open surface that to the cultivated taste is among the most attractive features of the Park, can have any other use than that of a playground, and nothing is more certain than that the beauty of these lawns would soon be lost…if these games were to be constantly played upon them.…It would tend to depreciate the attractions of the Park to the far greater number who visit it for the refined pleasures that its landscape affords to those who are sensitive to natural beauties.… And this use is not to be diminished to accommodate sports, of themselves innocent and worthy of encouragement, but participated in by comparatively few persons."

Olmsted's argument has as much to do with social class as it does with the quality of the park's lawns. Although the upper classes enjoyed tennis in the park, the majority of ballplayers to whom Olmsted was referring were middle- and working-class people. His assertions that those with "cultivated tastes" prefer green lawns to athletic fields and that rural landscape affords "refined pleasures" to those who are "sensitive" to such things betrays a classism with which one might well take issue. The reformers certainly did, although their assessment of what the city's poor needed may be criticized for its similarly prescriptive point of view.

Perhaps more than the growth of organized sports, it was the advent of the automobile that most dramatically changed

The sapling elm trees planted at the Mall quickly grew to form a canopy above the formal promenade.

the face of the park. The first cars arrived in New York City in the 1890s, and the first auto race was held on May 30, 1896. By the summer of 1899, Central Park was the only park to have banned cars from appearing inside the perimeter wall. Protests by the Automobile Club of America eventually relaxed the rule. A seven-mile-per-hour (11.2 kph) speed limit (three and a half mph [5.6 kph] when near carriages or pedestrians) discouraged fast driving, but the sport quickly gained great popularity. "Central Park," according to a 1926 report of a citizen's group called the Central Park Association, "had become Central Parkway."

In the teens and twenties, however, neglect posed an even greater threat to the park than the ballplayer or the automobile. The same report of the Central Park Association chronicled the decline: "For decades there have been no sound movement or efforts to improve the lawns, to plant trees in place of those which have gone, to renew the shrubbery, to fertilize the Park, to bring in new life, to improve and enlarge the system of drainage, to put an end to littering and vandalism, to do any other useful and constructive thing including the development of the public respect and affection for the City's most valuable possession."

Citizen groups rallied on behalf of the park, but to little avail. In 1904, the Parks and Playground Association of the City of New York was formed to defend the park against the twin evils of encroachment and neglect. A decade later, the Parks Conservation Association was formed, made up of "leaders of more than forty civic organizations…to marshall the representatives as commanding officers of the army of defense." In 1926, this organization gave birth to the Central Park Association, which despite the efforts of many, could not save Central Park.

Responsibility for the woeful neglect of Central Park fell on the shoulders of Tammany Hall. Park jobs were still political rewards, and the department's 1932 expenditures tell this story best. Of a total park budget of $8,576,319, only $225,000 was spent on materials and equipment. The balance paid salaries and bought Tammany votes.

The election of Fiorello LaGuardia in 1934 finally broke the back of Tammany Hall, and with LaGuardia as mayor, Central Park won a powerful advocate. He unified New York's five parks departments (one per borough) and handed the reins to Robert Moses, who had, among his other accomplishments, built Long Island's first parkways and created Jones Beach. Moses' biographer, Robert Caro, describes the devastation that the new parks commissioner inherited.

The park's lawns, unseeded, were expanses of bare earth, decorated with scraggly patches of grass and weeds, that became dust holes in dry weather and mud holes in wet. Its walks were broken and potholed. Its bridle paths were covered with dung. The once beautiful Mall looked like the scene of a wild party the morning after. Benches lay on their backs, their legs jabbing at the sky. Trash baskets had been overturned and never righted; their contents lay where they had spilled out. The concrete had been stripped off drinking fountains so completely that only their rusting iron pipes remained. And nine out of every ten trees on the Mall were dead or dying.

In one remarkable year, 1934, Moses cleaned up Central and other New York parks. Flowers bloomed where there had been bare dirt, the park wall was sandblasted to its original dark cream color, and lawns were reseeded, walks repaved, and drinking fountains repaired.

Nineteen thirty-four was also the year that Moses razed one restaurant in Central Park and established another. On the east side of the park, Vaux had designed the Ladies Refreshment Salon, which for many years had offered tea and sandwiches to park visitors. In 1925, Mayor Jimmy Walker had blessed a $400,000 renovation that turned the salon into the Casino, a swanky night club and Tammany hangout. Moses, who hated Jimmy Walker, tore down the Casino in his first year as parks commissioner.

An infrared photograph of the park taken in the 1940s.

After the theatre

ETHEL MERMAN
STAR OF "ANYTHING GOES"
By arrangement with Vinton Freedley

LEO REISMAN
AND HIS ORCHESTRA

CASINO IN *Central Park*

LUNCHEON   DINNER
COCKTAILS   AFTER THEATRE

Cocktail Dansant Saturdays & Sundays

NO COVER CHARGE FOR DINNER GUESTS AT ANY TIME
Reservations: RHinelander 4-3034

*N*ighttime entertainment at the Casino (*above*) rivaled Broadway, as this *Playbill* advertisement indicates. The Casino was very popular at night (*right*). This photograph, taken from the top of the Naumburg Bandshell, is the work of the Parks Department's first photographer, Alajos Schuzler.

Across the park, however, Moses turned Jacob Wrey Mould's sheepfold into Tavern on the Green. An old friend of Moses, Arthur Schleiffer, became the restaurateur, and the Tavern opened on October 20, 1934. Meanwhile, the operator of the Casino, Sidney Solomon, took Moses to court. On the witness stand, Moses defended his action saying that only reasonably priced restaurants belonged in the park. Moses thought that lunch entrees should in all cases be less than a dollar and coffee no more than a dime. Solomon's attorney then handed him the menu for Tavern on the Green, which had entrees listed for more than a dollar and set the price of coffee at twenty-five cents.

Moses was parks commissioner for more than thirty years, but the remainder of his tenure didn't prove as glorious as his 1934 triumph. Although he did build a parks department larger than any before or after, Olmsted's vision was of little interest to Moses, who saw the need not for rural scenery but for facilities for active recreation. During his tenure, Central Park gained nineteen new playgrounds, twelve ball fields, handball courts, the Wollman Rink, the Tavern on the Green, and a reconstructed Central Park Zoo. Moses' political power enabled him to build as he pleased. Only once, when he planned to pave a new parking lot for the Tavern on the Green restaurant, did he meet resistance when a group of mothers who regularly used the threatened lawn thwarted his plans.

*T*he city's agreement with the current proprietor of Tavern on the Green (*above*) includes incentives to maintain and enhance the property, which may explain why the signature tree lights have become more elaborate. The interior of the Tavern has always been bright, like the decor of the early chartreuse room (*left*).

*R*obert Moses
(*left*) held centerstage as New
York City Parks Commissioner.
At this ceremony in 1943, he is
joined by Governor Dewey
(front row with legs crossed).

*C*urious New
Yorkers mobbed the Central
Park Zoo (*right*) on opening
day, December 12, 1934.

*M*ayor
LaGuardia presented former
governor Al Smith (*below*) with
his very own key to the zoo.

Robert Moses abdicated the parks commissionership in 1960. The Central Park he left behind no longer held the promise of 1934. One of Moses' greatest talents was procuring federal funds for park projects, but when that money was no longer available, the park was forced to survive on scraps from City Hall's table. The park's first one hundred years had seen many defenders rise up to challenge those who would spoil it, but the park could now only hint at the beautiful rural scenery envisioned by Olmsted and Vaux. Despite all of Moses' ideas and projects, the fabric of the park, its grass and trees and shrubbery, was dying.

New defenders of the park would in time make their stand. As Samuel Parsons predicted in 1918, "I still believe that the Park will eventually be restored to something of its pristine beauty....The New York American public will never allow their greatest treasure to pass entirely out of existence as a thing of beauty."

CHAPTER THREE

THE PARK SAVED

Central Park is one of the truly great urban spaces in the world, undoubtedly one of the greatest artistic achievements of American culture. It rates along with Moby Dick *and the creation of jazz as a new musical form. It also reflects a truly extraordinary act of political stamina. Central Park is a place where democracy, in a very real and personal way, flourishes every year; where people of all races and economic backgrounds have come together to enjoy life in the greatest city in the world.*

Gordon Davis
NYC Park Commissioner, 1978–1986

THE BIRTH OF THE CENTRAL PARK CONSERVANCY

By 1975, Central Park was in bad shape—just like New York City's finances. Park fixtures and furniture were broken and strewn about, lampposts were beheaded, and benches had lost their wooden slats. Olmsted's sweeps of green lawn had been trampled down, the soil so compacted that nothing could grow except puddles of water after a rain. Graffiti covered almost every available stone or wood surface. The park had a lawless look about it; it seemed unmanaged and unmanageable.

The park landscape had been battered in the 1960s with summer concerts and New Year's celebrations, peace rallies, and protest marches. But the same era had also brought new interest in the environment. The first Earth Day celebration

The towers of the San Remo apartment building on Central Park West are reflected in the Lake.

*B*etsy Barlow
Rogers spearheaded the
restoration of Central Park.

took place in April 1970, and as Americans began to think more and more about the land around them, a new generation of academics and urban planners began to remember Frederick Law Olmsted.

To mark the one hundred and fiftieth anniversary of Olmsted's birth in 1972, a group of enthusiasts formed the Olmsted Sesquicentennial Committee in New York and used the occasion to promote Olmsted's principles of park design, environmental conservation, and urban planning. That fall, the Whitney Museum of American Art mounted an exhibition entitled "Frederick Law Olmsted's New York," and a Wellesley- and Yale-educated Texan named Betsy Barlow (now Rogers) wrote the copy for the catalog. Rogers and the show's curator, William Alex, weren't the only scholars interested in Olmsted. Laura Wood Roper was writing his biography, and in Washington, D.C., Charles McLaughlin was editing what would be a five-volume set of Olmsted's papers.

Little did Betsy Rogers know that her work on the Whitney exhibition would be the beginning of a career devoted to Central Park. Although a well-established writer (her *The Forests and Wetlands of New York City* was nominated for a National Book Award in 1972), Rogers' role in the restoration of Central Park would be more practical than literary. Rogers had been a volunteer for the Parks Council, an advocacy organization for parkland throughout the city, but after a friend asked her to run a summer youth program in the park in 1975, she found the experience so compelling that she decided to focus her efforts specifically on Central Park.

"I couldn't believe," says Rogers, "that the city couldn't get itself together to save its premier park. I believed that the people who used it could save the park. So I started to raise a little money." When the summer program was over, Rogers stayed on at the Arsenal, the Parks Department headquarters, and became the executive director of the Central Park Task Force, which was funded by a group of women from some of New York's oldest families. The goals of the task force were to begin a planning process for the restoration of the park, to deliver volunteer programs for public schoolchildren, and to continue the summer program begun in 1975.

By 1978, the task force was fully incorporated. Support from the task force founders continued, the Exxon Corporation helped with the publication of *The Central Park Book*, and a $144,000 grant from the National Endowment for the Arts provided the organization's first paid staff.

But the volunteers of the Central Park Task Force were not the only citizens who had banded together to save the park. George Soros and Richard Gilder, investors who shared a deep commitment to the park, funded a management study and then formed the Central Park Community Fund to implement its recommendations. E. S. Savas, a professor of public systems management at Columbia University who had been a deputy mayor under John Lindsay, undertook the study and then joined the board of the community fund. The report included recommendations for improved management and policing of the park and for a restoration and regreening effort. It also pointed out that because the Parks Department divided responsibility by borough, no single executive coordinated work in Central Park. The report's suggestion that such a position be created proved the most important recommendation of the study.

In January 1978, Edward I. Koch became mayor of New York and appointed Gordon J. Davis his parks commissioner. Soros and Gilder were quick to present him with their management study, and at their urging, Davis began to look for an appropriate person to administer Central Park.

He did not have to look far. At an informal celebration ten years later, Davis described how he chose Betsy Rogers. "She invited me to dinner one night at her house, and during the course of the pot roast, as I dwelt on the issue of who should get this job, I looked up at Betsy and knew the answer. And so when she went to get the dessert, I followed her into the kitchen of her apartment, and it was almost like I was pro-

*Y*oko Ono Lennon points to a model of Strawberry Fields, the garden of peace she gave to New York City. With her is Mayor Edward Koch and Parks Commissioner Gordon Davis.

*T*he restoration of the East Green (*before and after, above*) turned this popular site at Seventy-second Street and Fifth Avenue from brown to green.

posing marriage. My hands were shaking. I said, 'Betsy, will you be the first Central Park administrator?'"

Rogers took the job in January 1979. Because of the city's straitened circumstances, there was no budget for the new projects and programs that would be required to turn the park around. A sponsors committee formed to fund the establishment of the Central Park administrator's office. Its members included Soros and Gilder, Joan Davidson of the J. M. Kaplan Fund, Arthur Ross, who was a task force trustee, Lucy G. Moses, a longtime park supporter, and Barnabas McHenry, who represented the interests of another generous donor, Lila A. Wallace. By late 1979, Davis and Rogers decided that the sponsors committee was not large enough for the job ahead and proposed the formation of a Central Park Conservancy.

The sponsors understood Central Park to be one of New York's major cultural institutions, an idea that Olmsted and Downing had believed strongly, but that had lost currency in the hundred years since the park was built. Now the sponsors were reclaiming that role for the park, and they were determined to build a board of prestigious New Yorkers that would place Central Park among the city's other major cultural institutions: the Metropolitan Museum, Lincoln Center, and the Public Library. Davis and Rogers met with several distinguished citizens in an attempt to find a chairman for the Conservancy, but had little initial success.

Fortunately, William S. Beinecke, the soon-to-retire chairman of Sperry & Hutchinson Company, walked into the park one afternoon and, noticing signs of landscape restoration in progress, expressed interest in what was going on. Rogers took him to meet Gordon Davis, and they persuaded him to become the Conservancy's first chairman.

Beinecke found his first and most important task an enormous challenge. "I went around that fall of 1980 recruiting a board of trustees. What did I have to sell? Nothing. Nothing except a sense of mission. Number one: Central Park is great to have around. Number two: It's rundown. Number three: It needs to be rebuilt." Although his appeals were to an elite, monied group of New Yorkers, Beinecke did not want the Conservancy to operate with a sense of noblesse oblige. "Central Park is for all citizens, and the Conservancy seeks to rehabilitate the park for all citizens. The Conservancy is not, must never be allowed to be, and should not be seen as an elitist organization of East Side snobs acting like Lord and Lady Bountiful. The Conservancy cannot *be* or *be regarded* that way, or it won't be effective."

The Central Park Task Force and the Central Park Community Fund folded into the new Conservancy. Richard Gilder, Joan Schwartz, and Arthur Ross represented the community fund on the new board, and Adele Auchincloss, Grace Hechinger, and Jason Epstein represented the task force. And Beinecke recruited new trustees: Lewis Bernard, Howard Clark, Robin Duke, Richard Gelb, Victor Marrero, and Basil Patterson. The new bylaws of the Conservancy called for three trustees to be appointed by the mayor, and Koch complied by naming Beinecke, Robert Morgenthau, and Franklin Williams as his designees. The group assembled for the Conservancy's first board meeting on December 4, 1980.

A MASTER PLAN FOR RESTORING CENTRAL PARK

The restoration of Central Park was already in progress by the time of the Conservancy's first board meeting. When Davis became parks commissioner, new bond guarantees enabled the city to once again fund capital projects in the park, and a team of young landscape architects were hired to draw up a plan. The Maine Monument at the park's southwest corner received its first face-lift. Wollman Rink, which Lewis Mumford had called an architectural disaster in 1951, began to undergo what would be a protracted renovation. New designs were drawn up at Davis' request to blend the rink more successfully into the landscape. The state pitched in as well by funding the resodding of the Sheep Meadow and installing an underground irrigation system.

State funds transformed the Sheep Meadow in 1979 (*before and after, above*). The new lawn stays healthy thanks to careful regulation of use by the Parks Department.

A winter's day at the Point in the Ramble shows a bare plot with graffiti-covered rock outcrops (*top*). The Conservancy planted berry-producing plants to help feed migratory and resident birds, removed the graffiti, and gave new life to this tiny peninsula in the Lake (*above*).

Private dollars added more restoration projects. A gift from the community fund had refurbished the interior of the Dairy, and the Victorian loggia, which had long since disappeared, was then rebuilt with city dollars. New gifts to the Conservancy funded the restoration of the fountains at Cherry Hill and Bethesda Terrace.

One of the city's projects was a two-million-dollar effort to dredge and relandscape the Pond at Fifty-ninth Street. Rogers described that project in a letter to the Conservancy trustees dated August 1981: "Since the design was done before the current Parks administration took office, it reflects more the landscape style of the followers of Robert Moses than that of our current plan, which is respectful of, if not an entirely literal application of, the design principles of Frederick Law Olmsted and Calvert Vaux."

"Our current plan," as Rogers described it, refers to work begun by the task force and continued by the Conservancy to develop a master plan for the restoration and management of Central Park. In April 1981, the Conservancy circulated a document entitled "Rebuilding Central Park for the 1980s and Beyond," which outlined the beginnings of such a plan. Over the next three years, creating the master plan would be the Conservancy's primary focus.

Not since Olmsted and Vaux had created their Greensward Plan had this tract of land been so carefully scrutinized. Rogers hired two of the landscape architects already working in the park, Marianne Cramer and Judith Heintz, to conduct or supervise ten separate studies that became the basis of the plan: architecture, hydrology, vegetation, soils, wildlife, maintenance and operations, circulation, use, security, and archives. Recommendations made by the plan support an Olmstedian restoration tempered by the need to serve modern visitors. "The idea," Rogers told a reporter in the spring of 1980, "is to be sensitive to Olmsted and Vaux, but to remember that the clientele now includes the road runners and rollerskaters. The Greensward Plan as Olmsted envisioned it has been seriously mutilated—and yet, it still works for twentieth-century people. Broken down as it is, the Park is still a great and ingenious work of landscape art."

The master plan's study of park use, undertaken in 1982 by William Kornblum and Terry Williams of the City University of New York, showed that 80 percent of park visitors come to Central Park for precisely the kind of experience that Olmsted intended to provide—respite and refreshment from the asphalt and concrete of the city. People-watching, relaxing, thinking, taking in the park, reading, and wandering were the six most popular activities of those surveyed.

The study of the park's circulation system, conducted by landscape architect and planner Philip Winslow, was a critical component of landscape design work for restoration projects. The pathways of the Greensward Plan focus more on guiding visitors south and north, than east and west. As the city grew up to surround the park, the need for east-west access increased. That, coupled with the addition of new recreation facilities, strained the original path system. Rather than coming to the park to enjoy a serpentine stroll through the scenery, many visitors now have a specific destination in mind and take shortcuts across the lawns to find the quickest route. As a result, ad hoc dirt trails, some of which the Parks Department has legitimized by paving, crisscross the landscape, creating a far more complex path system than Olmsted originally designed.

All of the studies laid the groundwork for the second half of the Conservancy's master plan, which contains recommendations for the restoration of specific park landscapes. Although a public hearing solicited opinions about the report's recommendations, the Conservancy never asked the city to approve the report as a whole. Instead, as individual restoration projects are designed and funded, the Conservancy submits them to a strict public review process that includes community boards, the Landmarks Preservation Commission, and the Art Commission. Presentations are also made to interested non-profit groups such as the Municipal Art Society and the Parks Council.

A rendering of Gapstow Bridge shows the Plaza Hotel in the background to the right. Missing is the GM Building that now dominates the Grand Army Plaza skyline.

Many of the restoration projects have been joint ventures of the city and the Conservancy. For example, Parks Department capital·funds paid for the restoration of Belvedere Castle, and the Conservancy raised money for the surrounding landscape. Often, the Conservancy will find designs for projects that are then incorporated into the city's capital construction schedule. A grant in 1986 funded design work for the restoration of the Harlem Meer. In 1990, public dollars funded the dredging of the Harlem Meer and the removal of the Moses-era concrete curbing. Private dollars then paid to plant a reestablished naturalistic shoreline and to build the Charles A. Dana Discovery Center.

Implementing the master plan meant focusing public and private resources on three tasks: rebuilding the park's architectural (both structural and landscape) heritage; regreening the park and providing consistent horticultural care for the park's meadows, woodlands, and gardens; and providing programs and security for park visitors. What follows are highlights of those goals.

REBUILDING CENTRAL PARK'S ARCHITECTURAL HERITAGE

In the picturesque areas of the park, Olmsted created rustic shelters, benches, and fences to complement the surrounding scenery. At one point, fifteen rustic summerhouses dotted the park. Usually located at high elevations, they afforded visitors seeking a resting place or shelter from sun or showers a magnificent view. These were fanciful Victorian structures, decorated with elaborate lattices of curved branches and roots. No original plans for these structures are known to exist, and it is thought that the skilled craftsmen who built them conceived the designs and used whatever wood was available to carry out their ideas.

In 1983, the Conservancy hired and trained a restoration crew to revive this lost art and its artifacts in Central Park. The crew lumbered unmilled cedar donated by property owners in northern Connecticut and upstate New York and learned traditional joinery techniques to fasten the wood together. The first projects were the wisteria pergola at West Seventy-third Street, the shelter in the Ramble, and the summerhouse in the Dene. Designs were painstakingly created from photographs of the original structures. When the restoration crew built the Cop Cot in 1984, they won a New York Architectural Award for their skillful accomplishment.

BRIDGES AND ARCHES

While one restoration crew learned how to fabricate rustic architecture, another crew began to restore the park's cast iron and masonry bridges.

No two of Central Park's thirty-six bridges and arches are alike. Five are cast iron; the most famous of these is Bow Bridge, which spans the Lake and connects Cherry Hill with the Ramble. Cast-iron technology became very popular in the 1860s, when forty-one cast-iron foundries operated in Manhattan and Brooklyn alone. Cast-iron bridges cost about one fifth of what masonry bridges cost, but Olmsted and Vaux were prompted by more than economy to choose this material. First, the strength of cast iron meant that the bridges could span longer distances with a grace and fluidity that complemented the natural curves of the landscape. Second, the material's pliability allowed the designers to add ornamental details of flowers and leaves.

Robert Moses removed two of the seven original cast-iron bridges and replaced broken wooden decking on others with poured concrete. Most of the original balustrades were lost.

*B*ow Bridge (*far left and left*) carries pedestrians from Cherry Hill to the Ramble. The detail at left shows wood decking and the intricate cast iron railing.

*B*ethesda Terrace was the one place in the park where Olmsted and Vaux intended to install a collection of sculpture. There were to be twenty-six statues and busts of famous Americans, but a lack of funds kept them from realizing their plans.

Thanks to Lucy Moses and Lila Wallace, Bow Bridge was restored in 1972; a decade later, Parks Department capital funds restored Pinebank Arch in the southwest corner and Bridges 27 and 28, which take joggers over the bridle path to the running track around the reservoir. In 1989, the Conservancy restored Bridge 24 at the southeast corner of the reservoir.

The Conservancy's highly skilled preservation crew has now become the city's contractor of choice. A series of city-funded and Conservancy-executed projects have continued the restoration of the park's bridges. Playmates Arch, which leads from the Dairy to the Carousel, was restored in 1989, and Driprock and Green Gap arches were completed in 1991.

Much of the sandstone balustrades of both Driprock and Green Gap needed replacement, and the search for matching sandstone led Conservancy craftsmen to the original source of the stone in New Brunswick, Canada. The quarry had not been open for a hundred years, but fortunately, the local stone company that owns the rights to the quarry was willing to reopen it. The new sandstone carvings are indistinguishable from the old.

BETHESDA TERRACE

Completed in 1864, Bethesda Terrace was one of the first structures built in the park. Its restoration was a top priority for the Parks Department and the Conservancy, in part because it has always functioned as the formal—and social—heart of Central Park.

Olmsted described the Terrace as an "open-air reception hall." Designed by Vaux and another architect, Jacob Wrey Mould, the elaborately balustraded upper terrace, the sculptured double staircase, the broad plaza below, and the graceful bronze fountain form the architectural highlight of Central Park.

One hundred years of wind, water, ice, pollution, tree roots, and human abuse had left their mark on the Bethesda Terrace. By the late 1970s, roots had displaced large stones and topsoil had washed down the slopes and collected against the side walls of the Terrace. Wind and weather had worn away many of the details in the sandstone carvings of fruit and flowers, birds and vines. Vandals had broken off pieces of the carvings and defaced the walls and balustrades with graffiti.

The design of the Terrace was intended to draw visitors down the staircase from the Mall, through the arcade decorated with a dazzling ceiling of colorful Minton tiles, and out onto the Terrace to the fountain and Emma Stebbins' *Angel of the Waters* statue. Or, visitors could linger on the upper terrace, looking out at the Lake and the Ramble, and then wander down one side of the double staircase that frames the arcade to the plaza below.

First to be restored was the angel statue. Installed in 1873, the statue illustrates the New Testament story of an angel bestowing healing powers on the pool of Bethesda in Jerusalem. The nineteenth-century reference was the Croton aqueduct, a magnificent engineering feat completed in 1842, which brought pure fresh water to New York City residents. The sculptor, Emma Stebbins, was the sister of the parks commissioner at that time, and her work was the first sculpture commissioned for the park.

The Bethesda Fountain (*below, left and right*) was the only sculpture commissioned for the construction of the park. The sculptor, Emma Stebbins, was the first woman to receive a commission to create a major work of art in New York City. Four putti, representing Temperance, Purity, Health, and Peace, stand below the upper basin of the fountain.

*B*oat traffic on the Lake (*right*) is nearly as congested as pedestrian traffic on the Terrace.

*R*estoring the staircase (*far left*) meant following the complex detailing (*left*) of Jacob Wrey Mould.

*A*ugustus Saint-Gaudens'
Sherman Monument was regilded in 1989.

City funds supplemented by private contributions funded the restoration, which began in August 1982, of the Terrace itself. The crumbling staircases were torn out and then reset. The original stonework was preserved as much as possible while new handcut stone from the original quarry in Nova Scotia replaced what had been too badly damaged. Expert stonemasons were called in to reset stones, repair and rebuild elaborate details, and carve the birds, fruit, flowers, and other ornaments that had disappeared.

When work began on the new concrete deck of the bridge, the serious condition of the original Minton tiles became all too clear. The primary problem was the attachment system: the iron backing on the panels had corroded from water and salt seeping from the bridge above. Realizing that the ceiling would at some point fall, workers carefully disassembled the tile panels and put them in storage. Ten years later, the 16,000 red and blue arabesque-patterned tiles are still awaiting private funding to make the reinstallation of the ceiling possible.

GRAND ARMY PLAZA

The idea for the Grand Army Plaza at the southeast corner of Central Park was conceived not by Olmsted but by a sculptor named Karl Bitter in 1898. Fifteen years later, an architect named Thomas Hastings won a design competition to carry out Bitter's idea. The design reflects the influence of the City Beautiful movement that began at the World's Fair in Chicago in 1893 and called for the construction of grand monuments that would inspire civic pride.

Grand Army Plaza is really two symmetrical plazas severed by Central Park South (Fifty-ninth Street). The Augustus Saint-Gaudens statue of Civil War General William Tecumseh Sherman stands on the northern plaza, facing south. On the southern plaza is the Pulitzer fountain, topped by a statue of Pomona, goddess of abundance, that faces north. Publishing magnate Joseph Pulitzer left money for the fountain in his will, perhaps prompted by his rivalry with publisher William Randolph Hearst, who had rallied public support for the construction of the Maine Monument at the park's southwest corner.

The limestone used for the Pulitzer fountain began to deteriorate as early as the 1930s, and the neglect of the 1970s hastened its decline. The Sherman statue was first gilded by the artist just before it was installed on its pink granite base in 1903. The monument was regilded in 1938, but by 1968, all of the gold leaf had worn off. In 1986, the Conservancy mounted a campaign to restore the plaza, the fountain, and the statue. By enlisting the support of the tenants and owners of the surrounding buildings, who were assessed a voluntary "window tax" based on the square footage of their office or building, the Grand Army Plaza Partnership raised $3.5 million for the restoration. A special gift funded the statue's restoration; it was regilded with 23.5 karat gold.

REGREENING CENTRAL PARK

When Betsy Rogers became Central Park administrator in 1979, there was only one gardener assigned to care for Central Park. The Conservancy hired a fledgling horticulture crew in 1981, and as of 1992, forty-six gardeners, forty-five of whom are paid by the Conservancy, care for the park's lawns, trees, shrubbery, and gardens.

In 1982, the Conservancy wrote a report assessing the park's horticultural condition. "There is not a corner of the Park where the trees and plants do not need attention, often emergency treatment. There is not an area of the Park where the soil does not need to be replenished or replaced." The Central Park Community Fund helped launch the park's first composting operation in 1979. At the Mount, which rises up behind the Conservatory Garden at East One Hundred and Fourth Street, several large mounds of decomposing leaves provide 5,000 cubic yards of organic matter that help to enrich the park's depleted soil.

In order to ensure the future maintenance of Central Park and to secure the public and private investment in its restoration, the Conservancy started an endowment fund for the

The restored Pulitzer Fountain (*above*) is now ringed with trees and colorful planting beds.

The larger animals in the Central Park menagerie (*below*) were pressed into service to help mow park lawns (1863).

© Ted Hardin

The four rows of elm trees that line the Mall are part of the largest remaining stand of elms in North America.

park called the Greensward Trust. Interest from the endowment provides general funds to support the salaries of the park's gardeners. In some cases, individual landscapes have been endowed, assuring the presence of a full-time gardener to care for favorite areas. The Mall, Bethesda Terrace, Cherry Hill, the Conservatory Garden, the East Green, Conservatory Water, and Strawberry Fields are all tended by these "zone gardeners." The jobs offer skilled horticulturists a satisfying challenge: keeping three or four acres (1.6 ha) of Central Park in pristine condition.

As part of the work on the master plan, the Conservancy assembled a team of forestry students in 1982 to conduct the first comprehensive survey of all the trees in Central Park. The first tree was planted in Central Park on October 17, 1858. Over the years, Olmsted planted thousands more, many of which were unsuited to the park environment and have long since vanished. Others have flourished, however, including trees unknown in urban areas such as the beech. Today, Central Park boasts a grand collection of ailanthus, black cherry, oak, horse-chestnut, London plane, willow, and sugar, silver, red, Norway, and sycamore maples. Although fewer in number, its American holly, osage orange, gingkoes, Chinese elm, shingle oak, golden larch, bald cypresses, tupelo, and tulip trees are fine examples of their species. The team counted 24,600 trees and tabulated their size, species, and location in a computerized data base. That information enabled the Conservancy to create a five-year pruning cycle for 7,500 of the park's trees that, because of their value or location, require timely monitoring.

Even before the survey began, the first Conservancy foresters had begun to prune dead wood, brace limbs in danger of falling, and remove hazardous branches from pathways and playgrounds. And, to protect the park's 1,800 elm trees, a vigilant watch for signs of infection of Dutch elm disease began. Since the 1930s, Dutch elm disease has ravaged North America's elm population. The trees in Central Park are protected to some extent by the fortress created by Manhattan's buildings and the moat of rivers that surrounds the island. Until the Conservancy began to stand guard, an average of eighty Central Park elms died each year. In recent years, that number has dropped to the teens.

Neglect and the elm bark beetle were not the only threats to Central Park trees. The master plan's hydrology, vegetation, and soil studies pointed out the seriousness of the park's erosion and compaction problems. Pedestrian trampling had compacted the soil to such an extent that water and oxygen could no longer reach most tree roots. Rather than being absorbed by the soil, water ran over the surface, exacerbating erosion problems by carrying away precious topsoil and leaf litter. All of this debris ultimately made its way to the park's streams and lakes, which became smaller and shallower as a result.

The tree survey also produced a map of the park's tree canopy and compared it with the canopy of 1873. Hundreds of trees had been planted in the intervening years and even more had grown up on their own. Although Olmsted had intended a full canopy only in the Ramble, the north woods, and along the transverse roads and the perimeter, much of the park that was planned to be open meadow was now in shadow.

The density of the canopy became a contributor to the loss of groundcover plantings. In their work on the master plan, Marianne Cramer and Judith Heintz created a complete species list and map showing just how much of the park's ground plane was void of vegetation. Then, the Soil Conservation Service of the U.S. Department of Agriculture performed a soil survey, mapping soil types and explaining their characteristics and capacities for use.

The prognosis wasn't good. Only shade-tolerant plants could grow under the current tree canopy, and attempts to thin the park's trees to open the ground to sunlight had never been popular. In the beginning of the century, Samuel Parsons presented plans to do this and was met with strenuous opposition. Only when he submitted his proposal to three nationally recognized experts assembled by the press

Snow rests on the elm branches, which make a tangled pattern against the sky.

did public opinion allow him to proceed. The experts had approved of his plans but recommended that twice the number of trees be removed.

Central Park's woodlands are not only a picturesque retreat for city dwellers—they provided a habitat for wildlife as well. Although the white-tailed deer, gray wolves, black bears, bobcats, beavers, wild turkeys, and ruffed grouse that roamed Manhattan in the seventeenth century had long since departed, the master plan wildlife study turned up some surprises. Muskrats, woodchucks, raccoons, bats, eight species of fish, unusually large crayfish, turtles, frogs, and fresh-water jellyfish inhabit Central Park. Bird-watchers had long known that Central Park is a favorite stopover for migratory birds. An island of green along the Atlantic flyway, Central Park has hosted more than 250 species of birds, forty-two of which reside there permanently.

In 1989, the Conservancy hired an environmental consulting firm to assess the deteriorated state of the park's 130 acres (53 ha) of woodlands. Pedestrian trampling, compaction, and erosion of the soil, and the aggressive self-seeding species such as Norway maples and Japanese knotweed were threat-

Before the Heckscher Ballfields were restored (*above, left*), there was no grass and very poor drainage. Today (*above, right*), these ballfields are among the most sought after in the city.

ening the woodland's health and diversity. The restoration of urban woodlands is a new field of research, and there were few models for the Conservancy to follow. Working with consultant Leslie Sauer, Marianne Cramer developed an incremental approach that stresses consensus-building and ongoing research of appropriate restoration techniques. In 1990, Cramer recruited a woodlands advisory board to direct the restoration of the Ramble, the north woods, and the Hallet Nature Sanctuary. Working in precise test plots, crews of volunteers excise young Norway and sycamore maples as well as Japanese knotweed. They then experiment with various erosion-control techniques and the planting of native wood floor species. By monitoring the test plots, the advisory board draws conclusions about the most effective restoration strategies.

© Sara Cedar Miller/Central Park Conservancy

*The rustic playground at East Sixty-seventh Street (*left*) was a gift of the Robert Wood Johnson family.*

PROGRAMS AND SECURITY FOR PARK VISITORS

More than three thousand volunteers now help the Conservancy and the Parks Department keep Central Park clean and green. The biggest annual spruce-up event, "You Gotta Have Park," began in 1983 when park enthusiast Jane Present came up with a way for the Conservancy to invite those who use the park to help take care of it. The result is a weekend festival in May with an army of volunteers clad in colorful T-shirts selling buttons for a dollar and painting benches and picking up litter throughout the park. Although hundreds of volunteers work in Central Park year-round, the "You Gotta Have Park" weekend spotlights their commitment.

Two Conservancy committees, the Perimeter Association and the Central Park Playground Partners, are organized by volunteers to raise money for park maintenance. The

© Sara Cedar Miller/Central Park Conservancy

*Volunteers of all sizes (*left*) participate in the Conservancy's annual spring cleanup, "You Gotta Have Park."*

Perimeter Association solicits the apartment buildings and hotels that surround the park to fund a four-man crew that circles the sidewalks just outside the park wall—along Fifth Avenue and Central Park North, West, and South—to pick up trash, close empty tree pits, repair the park wall, and maintain benches.

Similarly, the Playground Partners solicit parents who use park playgrounds to fund a crew dedicated to playground maintenance. The crew repairs play equipment, filters and replaces sand in the sandboxes, and helps keep the playgrounds clean. The Playground Partners also recruit volunteers for clean-ups in each of the park playgrounds.

Preparations for the master plan included a study of park security, but the subject was taken up again when the rape and brutal assault of a woman jogger in 1989 prompted the Conservancy to convene a citizens task force to assess park safety. The central insight of the latter study is that the volume of park use and the visitor's perception of his or her security go hand in hand: where visitors abound, people feel safe. The report's recommendations were therefore divided between structural issues such as better lighting, the installation of emergency telephones, and path work in the woodlands to improve vehicular access and park programs designed to increase the use of areas where few visitors venture. Most of those areas are in the upper park.

Central Park is statistically the safest precinct in New York City. When crimes occur, public reaction to them is strong, in part because Olmsted's conception of the park as an antidote to the urban experience has become the New Yorker's birthright. Crimes committed in Central Park not only violate the social contract, but they also violate the New Yorker's need to experience the park as an oasis and safe haven.

One of parks commissioner Gordon Davis' initiatives was to create a corps of urban park rangers, a force not unlike Olmsted's original park police. In 1981, private funding enabled the department to buy six horses and establish a corps of mounted rangers who, like the rangers on foot, give information and first aid and help enforce park rules through education. Federal funds from the Department of the Interior supplemented by a small match from New York state granted $800,000 to hire forty rangers and establish an environmental education program. Central Park's rangers first operated out of the newly restored Belvedere Castle.

Park security is also bolstered by volunteers who help make Central Park safe. Ever since the Second World War, the park has benefited from a corps of volunteers who form the Central Park unit of the auxiliary forces section of the police department. About seventy men and women volunteer to patrol the park every Monday and Wednesday from 8:00 P.M. until midnight and on the weekends from 9:00 A.M. until 5:00 P.M.

Two of the Conservancy's first projects were the removal of all graffiti in the park—a three-year project—and the design and installation of a new luminaire to top the park's 1,500 lampposts. The logic of making graffiti removal and improved lighting a top priority relied on an assumption that more than any other park-wide blight, graffiti and unreliable lighting make the park feel unsafe. On the other hand, fresh paint, clean masonry walls, and good lighting assert a strong management presence that discourages antisocial behavior and increases a sense of security. That premise has proven true again and again as new restoration projects are completed.

As the 1990 citizens task force report points out, nothing increases the perception of safety as much as the presence of other park users engaged in positive activities. The Conservancy learned this as early as 1980, when the restoration of the Dairy called upon park managers to decide its future use. Programming, they knew, was essential for securing

*T*he Central Park luminaire (*above*) brought Victorian charm and a new security strategy to Central Park in the early 1980s.

*O*nly gravity binds the boulders that form Huddlestone Arch, just west of Lasker Rink. The restoration of the arch and its surrounding landscape (*before and after, above*) made a dramatic difference in 1992.

the building, and they decided to convert the Dairy into a visitor center, with exhibitions on display and park maps and other information for sale. But without also creating formal programming, it would not attract enough visitors to make the building secure. That is why the Conservancy, drawing on the work of the Central Park Task Force, began to invite schoolteachers to bring their classes to the park for lessons in history, design, and environmental science. Two years later, Belvedere Castle reopened as the Central Park Learning Center, with programs initially provided by the urban park rangers and later by Conservancy staff. In 1992 alone, more than 12,000 students participated in conservancy education programs.

Bolstered by their early success, the Conservancy took on the derelict concert ground above Bethesda Terrace, home of the abandoned Naumburg Bandshell and a thriving narcotics trade. How could the Conservancy create a hub of positive activity at this site? The answer was SummerStage, a multicultural performing-arts series that drew an equally eclectic crowd to its free concerts. SummerStage music—from rap to mambo to gospel—dance, performance art, and literary readings are now an established tradition. When the restoration of the concert ground began in 1990, Summer-Stage moved permanently up the hill behind the bandshell to Rumsey Playfield.

The 1990 task force report observed that the upper park, particularly the area above the Ninety-seventh Street transverse road, received many fewer visitors than the lower park. For that and other reasons, it was perceived as less safe. The task force recommended the development of recreation programming to attract teenagers from the Upper West Side and Central and East Harlem to the upper park. And they identified the North Meadow Center, headquarters of the Parks Department's central communications office and the Manhattan urban park rangers and park enforcement patrol, as the best location for new programs.

In 1991, with new basketball courts built on half of the North Meadow Center's parking lot, the Conservancy's North Meadow recreation program began to enroll its first participants. Using the entire upper park as a recreational resource, the program now offers softball, tennis, swimming, basketball, skating, martial arts, dramatics, and rock climbing.

THE PUBLIC/PRIVATE PARTNERSHIP: A NEW PARADIGM FOR PARK MANAGEMENT?

The Central Park Conservancy is the first public/private partnership established on behalf of a municipal park. Its success has encouraged the formation of many similar groups. In New York City alone, there are now four non-profit organizations that were inspired by the Conservancy: the Prospect Park Alliance; the Riverside Park Fund; the Bryant Park Development Corporation; and the City Parks Foundation, which was founded by parks commissioner Henry Stern, who succeeded Gordon Davis in 1986, to raise money for the many neighborhood parks throughout the city and for major parks that have no conservancy of their own. Other groups from farther afield, determined to rescue parks in Chicago, Louisville, Boston, Montreal, and even Milan, Italy, have met with Rogers and her staff for advice.

*T*he Shakespeare Garden was neglected for years (*opposite*). The concrete lily pond was drained, and the garden was overgrown. The garden's restoration in 1988 (*left*) included the addition of rustic fencing and benches crafted by Conservancy crews.

The Conservancy's original mission was to restore the park from end to end. In twelve years, it has overseen a remarkable renaissance, thanks in part to the prodigious fundraising skills of its second chairman, James Evans, and the chairman of a successful fifty-million-dollar campaign, Henry Kravis. All of this private support has funded restoration projects, horticultural care, and programs for visitors. In 1990, a new fiscal crisis once again forced severe cutbacks in the Parks Department budget and increased the Conservancy's share of the Central Park operating budget to 55 percent.

Central Park, it seems, has been short-changed ever since it was first built: New York has never been able to provide the park with adequate funding for maintenance. In its earliest years, city politicians marveled at the tax revenues that sprung from rising property values at the park's perimeter. But those revenues were soon taken for granted, and the urgent need for parks and public space, strongly articulated by Bryant, Downing, Olmsted, and even Robert Moses, dropped from political consciousness. Other social problems press hard, but as the following chapters will attest, the health of Central Park—and, indeed, all parks—is of critical importance to the health of the city and its residents. How to fund Central Park's continued renaissance and the regreening of all urban parks deserves our urgent consideration.

CHAPTER FOUR

AN ARMCHAIR TOUR OF CENTRAL PARK

There is no better way to discover Central Park and enjoy everything it has to offer than to stroll through its woodlands and meadows, ramble around its playing fields and gardens, and explore its historical buildings and ornamental structures. Whether you're a New Yorker longing to log in a few more precious moments in the park or an out-of-towner saving up frequent-flier miles for your first visit to the Big Apple, here is a tour through the highlights and curiosities, both natural and architectural, of Central Park.

THE ARSENAL

The Arsenal is one of two buildings in Central Park that is older than the park itself (the other being the Blockhouse at One Hundred and Tenth Street). It was erected to replace a previous arsenal that was built downtown in 1808 and required the authorization of the state legislature to approve its construction on state land. The site, facing a thirty-acre (12 ha) area once known as Hamilton Square, was chosen because it overlooked the city to the south, it was suitable for gathering and reviewing troops, and it was conveniently located near the New York & Harlem railroad that crossed the square.

Groundbreaking for the building began on May 8, 1847, under considerable opposition. Many citizens feared the transfer of state arms and munitions so far uptown. "A city with a population of half a million," said an official repre-

A woman walks her dog amidst the quiet beauty of the snow-covered Mall.

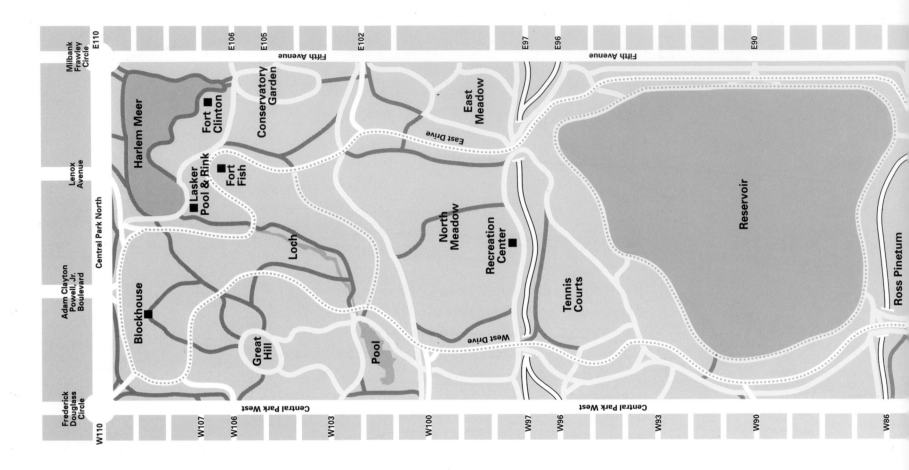

Key

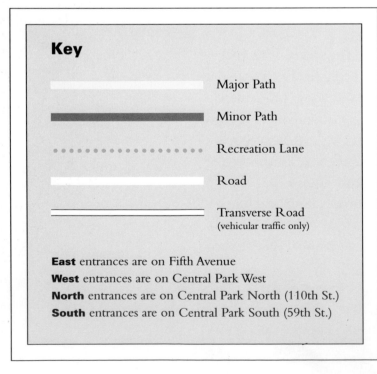

———————— Major Path

———————— Minor Path

• • • • • • • • • • Recreation Lane

———————— Road

———————— Transverse Road
(vehicular traffic only)

East entrances are on Fifth Avenue
West entrances are on Central Park West
North entrances are on Central Park North (110th St.)
South entrances are on Central Park South (59th St.)

Sites to See	Street Reference
Alice in Wonderland Statue	East 75
Arsenal	East 64
Ballplayers House (Seasonal concession)	West 65
Belvedere Castle (Visitor Center)	West 79
Bethesda Terrace and Fountain	72, mid-Park
Blockhouse	West 109
Bow Bridge	West 73
Bowling Greens	West 69
Carousel	West 64
Cherry Hill	West 72
Chess & Checkers	64, mid-Park
The Conservatory Garden	East 103–105
Conservatory Water	East 73–75
Dairy (Visitor Center)	East 65
Delacorte Theater	West 80
East Meadow	East 97–100

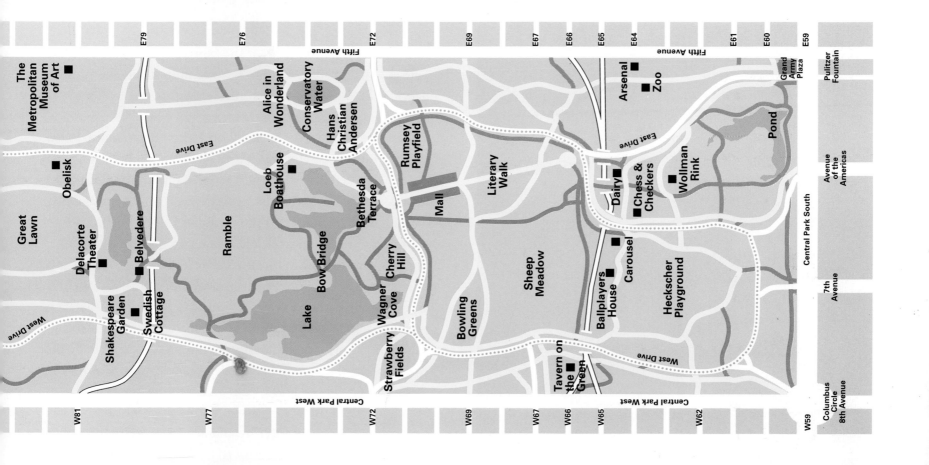

Sites to See	Street Reference
General Sheridan Statue	59 & 5th Ave.
Great Hill	West 105–106
Great Lawn	80–85, mid-Park
Harlem Meer	East 106–110
Hans Christian Andersen	East 74
Heckscher Playground	West 62–63
Lake	71–77, mid-Park
Lasker Pool/Rink	East 106–107
Literary Walk	East 66–67
Loch	102–106, mid-Park
Loeb Boathouse	East 74
Mall	East 66–70
Metropolitan Museum of Art	East 80–85
North Meadow Recreation Center	97, mid-Park
Obelisk	East 81
Pond	East 59–62

Sites to See	Street Reference
Pool	West 101–102
Pulitzer Fountain	59 & 5th Ave.
Ramble	74–79, mid-Park
Reservoir	86–96, mid-Park
Ross Pinetum	82–86, mid-Park
Rumsey Playfield	East 71
Shakespeare Garden	West 79–80
Sheep Meadow	West 67–69
Strawberry Fields	West 71–74
Swedish Cottage	West 79
Tavern on the Green	West 66
Tennis Courts	West 94–96
Wagner Cove	West 72
Wollman Rink	East 62–63
Zoo	East 63–65

The Arsenal is one of only two buildings in the park that predate the park itself.

tumultuous assemblages....If the cannons be all placed in the new Arsenal, distant four and a half miles from the present depot, they would be useless." Nevertheless, the building was completed in 1851, and the transfer was made.

With the pending design and construction of Central Park, the city purchased the Arsenal from the state. Although the Arsenal was a red brick structure with picturesque Norman towers, Olmsted and Vaux considered it to be an eyesore. "When we were preparing the design of Central Park," wrote Olmsted, "we advocated the retention of the building... because it would probably, if retained, be found to be of sufficient value to be converted into the nucleus of a museum, and although it was very inconveniently located for any such purpose, taking the proposed landscape of the park into consideration we felt that the opportunity was one that ought not to be lost." Olmsted and Vaux planted trees around the Arsenal that would grow into large enough specimens to soften its visual impact on the surrounding landscape. At the time, the Arsenal was the headquarters for the 11th police precinct. After the police moved out, a weather bureau was installed in an upper story in 1869. In the same year, the second and third floors became the first home to the New York chapter of the American Museum of Natural History.

In 1871, Boss Tweed had the Arsenal's facade covered with stucco and its turrets topped with pointed wooden towers. The park commissioners held office there until 1914 when they were transferred to the municipal building downtown, and in 1924, the building was renovated internally to accommodate the offices of the Parks Department. In 1934, parks commissioner Robert Moses ordered the stucco sandblasted off and the wooden towers replaced with concrete battlements. He also commissioned murals for the entrance hall. Today, the Arsenal still serves as the administrative headquarters for the Parks Department.

SHEEP MEADOW

Central Park boasts dozens of lawns, numerous fields, and countless grassy knolls, but perhaps none is more popular for the decadence of daydreaming and the indulgence of inactivity than Sheep Meadow, the twenty-two-acre (8.8 ha) lawn that stretches from the West Drive to the Mall at Sixty-seventh Street. This wealth of lush green grass at the heart of the park is testament to the park managers who not only maintain the lawn but also keep it restricted from organized sports. Such rigid guidelines regarding its use, however, are fairly recent.

In 1857, the Central Park commissioners insisted that all entries in the design competition for the park include an area for military exercises. Olmsted and Vaux's design set aside an area they called the parade ground. Before construction was completed, however, military displays were banned from the park. The result was a meadow populated—intentionally— with a flock of Southdown sheep. The inspiration probably stemmed from William Gilpin, the eighteenth-century landscape theorist who had written, "Sheep particularly are very ornamental in a park. Their color is just that dingy hue, which contrasts with the verdure of the ground; and the flakiness of their wool is rich and picturesque."

The sheep were housed in a building to the west of the grounds (now incorporated into Tavern on the Green) and twice a day a park shepherd held up traffic on the West Drive as he ushered the animals to and from the meadow. For almost sixty years, the sheep gathered in the parade ground meadow, until practicality won over aesthetic value and parks commissioner Robert Moses had them removed for health reasons in 1934.

Despite the original intention of using the meadow location as a parade ground, Olmsted and Vaux were determined to give primary importance to the landscape design of the area and only secondary importance to any necessary structural features. This was accomplished by designing a row of trees along the meadow's edges that produced a living border

The original inhabitants of Sheep Meadow, circa 1895 (*top*), before they were ousted for health reasons in 1934. Sheep Meadow is now (*above*) one of the most popular destinations for picnickers and sun worshipers.

*O*lmsted and Vaux purposely located the Mineral Springs Pavilion on the perimeter of Sheep Meadow so that it wouldn't disrupt the integrity of the rolling green lawn and the border of surrounding trees.

that became blurred in a combination of light and shadow. Their intentions were also reflected in the Mineral Springs Pavilion, an elaborate cast-iron octagon that was erected on the perimeter of the grounds at the northeast corner of the meadow. The pavilion acted as a concession to the meadow grounds, serving thirty different kinds of mineral water from the bar within. It became known as "Little Carlsbad" during its existence, but when the taste for mineral water evaporated, the structure reverted to a storehouse and was eventually demolished in 1960. A second concession building—still standing—was erected east of the original under Robert Moses' direction.

In the 1960s and 1970s, the meadow came under heavy use as a site for concerts, rallies, and recreational sports, and the result was compacted soil and turf that was completely ruined. In 1979, the meadow was reconstructed. Thanks to a new restriction on athletic activity, the meadow remains lush and green today, a mecca for sun worshipers who seek safe haven from the competitive playfulness in other areas of the park.

THE RAMBLE

One of the many goals of the original park plan was to create a balanced design, with equal parts of open meadow, sculptured walkways, romantic bodies of water, and wooded terrain. The first landscape that Olmsted and Vaux built was the Ramble, thirty-three acres (13.3 ha) of woodland wilderness in the middle of Central Park that ran from the East Drive to the West Drive and from the Lake to the Seventy-ninth Street transverse.

The Ramble was planned to look unplanned, and one of the greatest compliments it received was from Horace Greeley, who, having toured the newly completed Ramble, declared, "Well, they have let it alone a good deal more than I thought." Nothing was further from the truth. The designers lavished attention on the Ramble. No other section of the park can match the Ramble's intricacy, variety, and elaborateness of detail.

The twenty-acre (8.1 ha) Lake, which wraps around the Ramble on the south and west sides and borders Bethesda Terrace, was built out of a swamp. Originally, the Lake covered a slightly larger area, including two and a half miles (4 km) of shoreline and an arm of water called the Ladies Pond. When a malaria scare gripped the city in 1880, part of the Ladies Pond was filled in as a concession to those who warned that the water bred deadly mosquitoes. In 1934, Robert Moses finished the job.

In its various sizes, the Lake has always been used for pleasure boating. At first, boats provided passengers with scenic tours, stopping at any one of six boat landings to let people on or off. Later, park visitors propelled themselves in everything from rowboats to swan boats to gondolas. The six original boat landings have disappeared over time, but four new ones have been built to let voyagers stop and rest on their journey around the Lake.

Meandering through the heart of the Ramble is the Gill, a thousand-foot (304 m) ribbon of water that slips through quiet woods and under paths and bridges as it makes its way to the Lake. The three small original bridges that at one time crossed the Gill are now gone—one was replaced by a well-crafted rustic replica in 1984, one by a pipe rail-and-cement structure that was constructed in 1935, and one by a wooden bridge.

The source of the Gill, in the middle of the Ramble, leads immediately to the Azalea Pond. Not only does this pond host some of the oldest plants in the park—azaleas that may be well over one hundred years old—but it also provides shelter for some of the more uncommon birds that grace the Ramble, including ruby-throated hummingbirds that sip the nectar of the azaleas, and cardinals who play in the surrounding bushes.

Despite its present-day appearance as a completely natural landscape, the truth is that the Ramble was painstakingly constructed out of a swamp. This view looks west toward Balcony Bridge.

The Ramble was once home to six prominent ornate bridges. Bow Bridge, one of only two that are still intact, is an elegant cast-iron structure that was erected in 1859–60. Designed by Vaux, Bow Bridge mixes classical Greek detailing with more lavish Renaissance ornamentation. Like other cast-iron works in the park, use, abuse, and lack of funding over time led to the bridge's disrepair. By the 1970s, Bow Bridge was crumbling. It was saved from collapse by generous donations from Lila A. Wallace and Lucy G. Moses and was completely restored in 1974. Today, the gentle ballooning shape and pale wood of Bow Bridge reflects wonderfully off the water it spans between the Ramble and Cherry Hill.

*B*ow Bridge, spanning the Lake between the Ramble and Cherry Hill, is one of six ornate bridges originally constructed in this area of the park. Today, only two are still standing.

The Ramble was also resplendent with rustic architecture, a typical component of the English Landscape School's picturesque setting. More than a half dozen rustic shelters once dotted the Ramble. From large pavilions to fanciful bird-houses and beehives to the guide rails that used to protect the Ramble landscape, these rustic pieces offered both aesthetic value and useful purpose. Today, the last remaining original rustic structure is a shelter located to the north of Bow Bridge. It was built in 1863 and is made from mature red cedar, which is resistant to rot and insects.

Over the years, mismanagement and insufficient funding took a very evident toll on the Ramble. In the original construction of the area, Olmsted and Vaux included a cave and a waterfall. The waterfall, near the mouth of the Gill, consisted of a series of rocks that were positioned to form a "natural" rockslide, with water gushing over them and a stone bridge passing directly above. A hundred feet from the waterfall, there was a cave that could be entered by rowboat from the water or by a set of steps cut into the adjacent slope. By the 1930s, the stone bridge had deteriorated so significantly that it was replaced with one made from concrete, and the rambling stream was diverted through the base of the rocks instead of over their peak. The cave, meanwhile, was sealed for safety reasons, and the inlet leading to the cave has since been silted in with soil drained down from the surrounding slopes.

The Ramble has always been a particular mecca for New York bird-watchers. Many of the 259 species of birds that have been spotted in the park can be found in the Ramble, which remains an important stop on the north-south migratory flyway, especially so because the northeast corridor continues to lose green way stations for birds to rest and refuel before continuing their journey. Additionally, the Ramble is dotted with sixty quality trees, including Kentucky coffee trees, cork trees, cucumber magnolias, and Japanese pagoda trees. Tupelo, sweet gum, and red maple have flourished in the flatter, wetter areas, and the Point and Gill are covered with dense plantings of seed- and berry-producing shrubs that provide food for migratory birds and a secluded haven for Sunday strollers.

*B*oth boaters and strollers can appreciate the elegant design and graceful lines of Bow Bridge.

THE ZOO

There are very few places in New York that offer as much fun and excitement for children as the Central Park Zoo. Nestled behind the Arsenal on the east side of the park at Sixty-fourth Street, the zoo was not a part of the park's original design but has been a constantly changing piece in the Central Park puzzle.

In 1859, one year after work officially started on the park, a bear cub was presented to city hall commissioners in appreciation of the great "wilderness" that they had brought to New York. A man named Phillip Holmes was designated the bear's keeper, and he became the first zookeeper of the first animal in the first zoo in the nation. For many years, Olmsted and Vaux resisted pressure to include a proper zoo in the park plans. Four separate sites were considered at various times, but in each instance, work was started and ultimately abandoned.

Meanwhile, the animal gift-giving continued. Grazing animals were considered an aesthetically pleasing addition to any landscape, and as a result, a deer paddock was formed on the grounds to the east of the Mall. In the northern reaches of the park, a pasture was dedicated to horned cattle, and the inhabitants included moose, African buffalo, and beef cattle from England, Ireland, and Spain. Eagles, foxes, and prairie dogs were donated to the park. Eventually, the commissioners were forced to set up a makeshift menagerie in the basement of the Arsenal and later in a succession of wooden sheds outside.

To the park officials' great surprise, these new structures proved enormously entertaining to Central Park visitors. Beginning in 1870, the menagerie attracted nine out of ten people who entered the southern end of the park. In fact, the animals were so popular among New Yorkers from all walks of life that the park was soon hosting crowds with far more diverse interests. No longer was the sole purpose of the park a genteel stroll or even a zip around a skating pond; these animals were the park's first "attraction."

By 1932, city hall was accepting all manner of creatures great and small—including pumas, baboons, and tigers—all in varying degrees of health, with many suffering from poor handling and mistreatment by their previous owners. The Central Park "zoo" became a sort of repository for wayward beasts. To worsen the problem, the wooden structures containing the animals were decrepit and crumbling. It was not until Robert Moses became the parks commissioner that the animals' inadequate housing was addressed. In 1934, under the guidance of Moses, a spanking new zoo was erected. A U-shaped border of attractive red brick and white limestone buildings surrounded a central sea lion pool. The new design was praised for its careful planning and thoughtful design, and again the zoo became the most frequently visited feature in the park.

In 1960, in an effort to create a recreational attraction for the children of the city, Governor and Mrs. Herbert H. Lehman donated the buildings that comprise the present

*C*onstruction-in-progress (*left*) on Robert Moses' "new" zoo in 1934.

*I*n Moses' original design (*right*), as well as in the current zoo, the sea lion pool is the center of all activity.

Children's Zoo. The buildings were all designed as Disneyland-style nursery-rhyme settings, located in the triangle of land just north of the Moses Zoo formed by the entrances to the Sixty-fifth Street transverse. In 1965, George Delacorte donated the chiming clock that crowns the facade of the southern zoo gate with a sextet of animals playing musical instruments.

Almost from the moment that Moses' zoo was finished, a controversy arose. Some people praised the design for its aesthetic appeal while an equal number criticized its lack of humaneness: the caged animals had no room to move about freely or run around, the cells had no padded sleeping areas, and the animals were usually restricted to solitary confinement. More importantly, the passing of the decades showed the general public that solid structures alone could not keep the animals healthy. By the 1980s, it was clear that attention to the nutritional needs and veterinary care of the zoo's inhabitants was woefully inadequate.

In 1984, the New York Zoological Society—overseers of the famous Bronx Zoo and New York Aquarium—took over as managers of the Central Park Zoo. Their first task was to resettle the existing animals—more than one hundred and fifty of them—to other zoos around the country while structural modifications were taking place. They were then faced with the challenge of renovating property that was not only designated a historic landmark but was part of a public park as well. Many compromises were worked out, including retaining the old zoo plan, centered on the seal pool, while placing all the major exhibits to the west of the walkway behind the Arsenal in order to accommodate the heavy pedestrian traffic. The results were enormously successful. Not only is the redesigned zoo a model of advanced architectural technique, incorporating elements of the surrounding cityscape into the zoo's buildings, but it is also a major step forward for the animals because they are separated into "habitats" that seek to duplicate their native environment.

The zoo today is divided into three areas: the polar circle, the temperate territory, and the tropic zone. Each is designed with its own climate, its own vegetation, and its own indigenous animals. Gone are the days of lions and elephants pacing back and forth in their cages: the zoological society decided that a tiny zoo situated in the middle of a major metropolitan area like New York could not sustain the needs of such animals. In their place, however, came sea otters, Asian deer, and red pandas of the temperate territory; flying geckos, lizards, and parrots that live in the thick mist of the tropic zone; and snowy owls, puffins, and penguins that inhabit the polar circle. Two animals take center stage in the new zoo: The polar bears now have a micro-climate-controlled enclave surrounded by Plexiglas that allows visitors to watch them roam freely both above and below water, and the seals and sea lions have a new raised tank with Plexiglas sides in the middle of the zoo courtyard that also allows spectators to observe activity below the water's surface.

The existence of a zoo in the heart of Manhattan is a precious and rare commodity. The history of the Central Park Zoo speaks to the danger and precarious nature of such an undertaking, where the vagaries of city budgets are potentially more damaging to animals than they are to park landscape. With the support of New Yorkers and the New York Zoological Society, the park has the potential to remain a proud host for generations to come.

$\mathcal{T}$he Delacorte Clock (*far left*), marking the entrance to the zoo at the southern gate, chimes every hour with the help of an orchestra of animals with a repertoire of thirty-two different nursery rhymes.

$\mathcal{T}$he design of the current zoo (*left*) takes advantage of modern materials and innovative construction techniques to provide a healthier habitat for the animals as well as a better perspective for zoo visitors.

$\mathcal{F}$eeding time at the zoo (*above and left*) is greeted with almost as much enthusiasm from spectators as from the animals.

THE OBELISK

There is no single structure more curious and more out of place in Central Park than the obelisk that stands on the grassy knoll just west of the Metropolitan Museum of Art on East Eighty-first Street. The obelisk was a gift to the United States in the late nineteenth century, but its history stretches much further back.

Known for a time as Cleopatra's Needle, the obelisk in fact had nothing at all to do with the Egyptian queen. The obelisk's history began around 1500 B.C. (roughly 1,400 years before Cleopatra's rule), when Thutmose III, the ruler of Egypt, commissioned the obelisk to mark the fourth anniversary of his reign. Cut from a single piece of red granite at the quarries near Aswan in southern Egypt, the obelisk is seventy feet (21 m) high and weighs 225 tons (204,075 kg). The monument was taken by barge 600 miles (960 km) down the Nile to the ancient city of Heliopolis (near present-day Cairo), where it was placed in front of the sun temple alongside a companion obelisk (later moved to the bank of the Thames River in London).

In 12 B.C., Caesar Augustus moved the obelisk to Alexandria, where it remained until 1869. That year, at the celebration

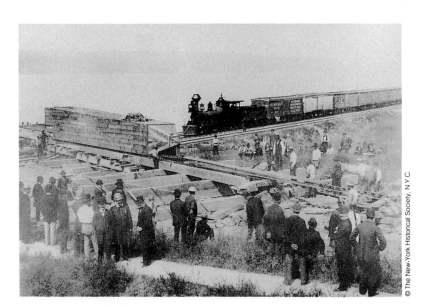

commemorating the opening of the Suez Canal, the king of Egypt presented the obelisk as a gift to the United States. A site was eventually chosen in Central Park near the Metropolitan Museum, and William Vanderbilt offered to pay all transportation expenses. The logistics of moving the obelisk to New York were left to Lieutenant Commander Henry H. Gorringe of the U.S. Navy. In October 1879, Gorringe sheathed the obelisk in protective planking and lowered it through a makeshift opening into the hold of a dismantled Egyptian postal steamer. The voyage from Alexandria to New York City took thirty-eight days.

Since no dry dock company in Manhattan would make its facilities available at an affordable price, Gorringe unloaded the obelisk on Staten Island. It was then attached to pontoons and floated upriver to West Ninety-sixth Street. From there, a specially constructed railway carried the obelisk south to Eighty-sixth Street through Central Park along the transverse road to Fifth Avenue and finally to Eighty-second Street where a wooden trestle carried it to the park site. The trip through Manhattan alone took 112 days. The formal presentation to the city took place in front of a crowd of twenty thousand on February 22, 1881.

*T*ransporting the obelisk (*left*) from West Ninety-sixth Street to its final resting place in Central Park (*far left*) required 112 days and a specially constructed railway.

*W*hile historians try to determine how to stop the slow deterioration of the thirty-five-hundred-year-old obelisk itself (*right*), the Central Park Conservancy has renovated and relandscaped the area around the base of this treasure. The plaques that translate the obelisk's hieroglyphics were a gift of Cecil B. deMille.

𝒯he Three Dancing Maidens by sculptor Walter Schott (*left*) has graced the Conservatory Garden's north garden since 1947.

𝒯he Italianate central courtyard of the Conservatory Garden in full bloom (*opposite*).

THE CONSERVATORY GARDEN

The thought of Central Park conjures up images of rolling lawns, ball fields, and thick woods, but very few people know that one of the finest formal gardens in the United States is located in Central Park. The Conservatory Garden, just off Fifth Avenue on One Hundred and Fifth Street, is one of New York City's best-kept secrets and is well worth discovering.

In keeping with Olmsted's vision of a park for all New Yorkers, the original Greensward Plan included a formal garden at the southern end of the park, accessible from both Fifth Avenue and Bethesda Terrace, which would serve as a major social meeting area. The garden was designed to sit twenty feet (6.1 m) below the level of Fifth Avenue, so that the public could have a clear and sweeping view of the geometric design of flower beds. A glass conservatory was to be built, with a reflecting pool to mirror the seasonal display of flowers. Unfortunately, the nursery that offered to supply all

the trees and plants for the garden never fulfilled its promise, perhaps due to a lack of city funds, and the design was never realized. A reflecting pool was built, however, and in memory of the original plan, it is known as Conservatory Water.

In addition to a formal garden, the Greensward Plan also included an arboretum located in the northern end of the park. Olmsted felt strongly that bold patches of flowers and unique trees would command too much attention from park visitors and would disrupt the carefully planned vistas and natural beauty of the rest of the park. Therefore, he proposed that a section of the upper park away from the main thoroughfares but still accessible to park visitors would serve as the site for this garden of trees. Olmsted wanted to illustrate the unique beauty of many of North America's indigenous species and sought to use the arboretum as a learning environment for interested visitors. Unfortunately, the arboretum proved unfeasible, and greenhouses and a nursery were built instead. In 1899, a glass conservatory (like the one

Olmsted intended for the south end of the park) was built on the site at One Hundred and Fifth Street. From the start, it was an extremely popular tourist attraction. More than a dozen gardeners worked at the conservatory, growing plants for parks around the city and maintaining an outstanding botanic collection. However, due to the rising cost of maintenance, the conservatory was torn down in 1934, and the current Conservatory Garden was laid out in its place.

Parks commissioner Robert Moses commissioned the Conservatory Garden as a W.P.A. project to provide employment during the Depression. The original planting plan was designed by Betty Sprout, a landscape architect for the Parks Department, and the garden was officially opened to the public in 1937. The garden is divided into three sections: the north garden, built in a circular pattern after the French parterre style and planted with tulips and chrysanthemums; the south (or secret) garden, designed in a more intimate style of concentric horseshoe shapes and planted with perennials; and the center garden, a rectangular lawn framed by yew hedges and crab apple allées. Fountains decorate each of the three gardens, and an ornate French iron gate that used to grace the Vanderbilt Mansion on Fifty-eighth Street now welcomes visitors at the Fifth Avenue entrance to the garden.

In 1982, after forty-five years of service, the Conservatory Garden underwent major restoration at the hands of the Central Park Conservancy. Graffiti was cleaned from fountains and benches, trees and shrubs were pruned or removed, new flowers were planted, and most importantly, a full-time gardener was hired. In 1987, the Weiler-Arnow family endowed the garden with a gift of $1.5 million, ensuring its permanent care. The 1982 user survey identified the garden as the second most avoided landscape in the park. Today it is one of the most popular, attracting both park neighbors and tourists. It is a favorite spot for wedding pictures and also hosts school programs and musical and dramatic performances.

*R*ainbows and sunshine (*opposite, top*) are only modest additions to the spectacular natural display of floral colors in Conservatory Garden.

*T*he Vanderbilt Gate (*right*), formerly of the Vanderbilt Mansion at Fifth Avenue and Fifty-eighth Street, now graces the entrance to the Conservatory Garden on Fifth Avenue and One Hundred and Fifth Street.

*A*t the center of the English-style garden at the southern end of the Conservatory Garden is a statue honoring Frances Hodgson Burnett (*opposite, bottom*). The two figures of a young boy and girl are taken from her children's book, *The Secret Garden*, from which the garden gets its name.

*T*he *Imagine* medallion (*above*) that greets visitors to Strawberry Fields is a black-and-white marble reproduction of an original Pompeian mosaic.

*S*trawberry Fields (*below*) was designed as a "garden of peace," planted with trees from all over the world.

STRAWBERRY FIELDS

In 1981, following the death of former Beatle John Lennon, the mayor and the city council of New York passed a resolution to dedicate a portion of Central Park to his memory. The spot chosen was a tear-shaped, two-and-a-half-acre (1 ha) meadow located just inside the Women's Gate at West Seventy-Second Street. The area, across the street from the famed Dakota building where Lennon lived, had been the favorite oasis of John and his wife, Yoko.

Through a generous gift to the Central Park Conservancy from Yoko Ono Lennon, a landscape restoration plan was developed and implemented. Olmsted and Vaux originally designed this area to be broad and open without the interference of crossing paths or decorative elements. Landscape architect Bruce Kelly's design for the area, which was renamed Strawberry Fields in honor of Lennon, follows the 1873 plan of the park: an open meadow surrounded on three sides by deciduous trees and evergreen trees and shrubs. The restoration introduced 161 plant species—many were donated from countries around the world—and the landscape became a "garden of peace." Just a few of the garden inhabitants are American elms, ginkgoes, red twig dogwoods, and Dawn redwoods, as well as witch hazel, roses, rhododendrons, and even some strawberries.

In 1984 and 1985, community opposition erupted over the proposed installation of a mosaic in Strawberry Fields in memory of John Lennon. Local residents felt that such a "monument" would attract "undesirable fans" to the area. A compromise was finally reached, and in 1985, a black-and-white marble reproduction of an original Pompeian mosaic was installed into the footpath of Strawberry Fields. The single word in the middle of the starburst design, *Imagine,* is a reference to Lennon's song about world peace. Strawberry Fields was dedicated on October 9, 1985, and a gift from Yoko Ono Lennon has provided a permanent endowment for the area to keep it maintained year-round.

A simple plaque marks the entrance to the Shakespeare Garden, a "garden of the heart" that is planted only with flowers mentioned in Shakespeare's plays and poetry.

SHAKESPEARE GARDEN

There is a small patch of land wedged between the Swedish Cottage and the Delacorte Theatre on the west side of the park at Seventy-ninth Street that is home to one of Central Park's more charming and more obscure gardens. The Shakespeare Garden, with its irregular flower beds and winding paths, is one of Central Park's hidden jewels.

Originally established in 1912 as a "garden of the heart," a strictly Victorian expression from the late nineteenth century, the Shakespeare Garden has always maintained a truly romantic spirit. The original design included a shaded

bridge, narrow steps cut into the rock face, and flowing water leading to a series of descending pools. The intent was to make each level particularly mysterious, blocking off the view of certain flower beds from certain vistas, so as to make each stroll around the garden a journey of discovery.

In 1916, on the three-hundredth anniversary of Shakespeare's death, the management of the garden became the responsibility of the Shakespeare Society of New York City. Following a Victorian tradition, only flowers mentioned in Shakespeare's plays and poetry were planted in the garden.

The Shakespeare Society was unprepared to maintain the

garden during the Depression, so its management reverted to the Parks Department. During the Moses administration, pools were added to the garden, and the Parks Department maintained it until the fiscal crisis hit New York in the late sixties. At that time, the garden was all but abandoned until a group of volunteers, calling themselves the Shakespeare Gardeners, began the work of renovation and renewal in 1975. The paths were completely overgrown, and the flourishing weeds were choking what little life remained in the living trees and shrubs.

Beginning in 1975, most of the garden was carefully cleared. Once again, only the flora mentioned by Shakespeare was seeded. In 1987, restoration was taken one step further with a substantial gift from the Samuel and May Rudin Foundation. Landscape architect Bruce Kelly expanded the teardrop-shaped garden site to include the upper portion of the hill, and as a result, the garden was visually united with Belvedere Castle, which itself evokes the spirit and imagery of Shakespeare's plays. On June 1, 1989, the completely restored garden was dedicated.

Whether or not one chooses to revel in the Shakespearean imagery that permeates the garden's design, the plantings themselves provide a wealth of pleasure. From the abundant herbs planted in the central bed (including thyme, sage, savory, rue, rosemary, mustard, and chamomile) to the seasonal lilies, roses, violets, and pansies to the flowering magnolia and dogwood trees, the garden frames some of nature's simplest delights in the context of one of the world's greatest artists.

A bright swatch of yellow flowers decorates the grounds of the Shakespeare Garden.

THE POOL

There may not be another spot in the park that is more beautiful and yet gets less recognition than the Pool, a small two-acre (0.8 ha) body of water located near One Hundred and Second Street on the west side of the park.

Like the larger bodies of water in the park—the Lake, the Pond, and the Meer—the Pool was created by Olmsted and Vaux as part of their original design. On the south shore, specimen trees, including a bald cypress and a red maple, dot the gently rolling landscape. To the north, a meadow stretches halfway up the steep slopes of the Great Hill. The western edge is covered with dense foliage all the way to the park wall, and on the southeastern shore is a small beach that attracts ducks and geese.

To create the Pool, Olmsted and Vaux enlarged a stream, Montayne's Rivulet, to form a series of still pools linked by five (artificial) waterfalls. The Pool forms the head of this chain, and water descends from this source east to the Harlem Meer.

Ever since the Pool was completed, naturalists have appreciated the beautiful and varied vegetation that surrounds the banks. At one time, the Pool hosted European wood anemone, skunk cabbage, and Dutchman's breeches, dogwood, goldenrod, arrowwood, bog bilberry, ferns, cotoneaster, and spring beauty. Perhaps the single element that currently contributes most to the sense of tranquility and serenity in the area is the abundance of weeping willows surrounding the Pool.

A rustic bridge crosses the Loch (*above, right*), the stream that flows from the Pool to the Harlem Meer. The Central Park Conservancy has begun an effort to restore the Loch's waterfalls to Olmsted and Vaux's original design.

*T*his historic photograph of the Harlem Meer (*right*) shows the original naturalistic shoreline.

THE BELVEDERE

The Belvedere, or Belvedere Castle as it is commonly known, is one of the more curious and fanciful architectural elements in a park devoted primarily to rural landscape.

The rugged gothic tower of Belvedere Castle was designed by Calvert Vaux in 1867 and included in the original park plan as a romantic architectural folly and a focal point in the park's landscape. The Greensward Plan placed it atop a huge rock outcropping known as Vista Rock, one of the highest natural points in the park. This crescent-shaped foundation jutted into the southwest corner of the old Croton Reservoir and now anchors the same corner of Belvedere Lake (a much smaller body of water) close to West Eightieth Street. At the time of construction, the plan for the building, given its prominence in the park's landscape, was extravagant and expensive. However, after consulting with the architect Jacob Wrey Mould, it was decided that every unnecessary detail would be eliminated, including a second tower on the main structure, in order to make the construction more affordable. The castle was completed in 1872.

Since its opening, Belvedere Castle has served as the destination for thousands who stroll through the Ramble every year. Once there, they have the opportunity to climb over its terraces or up to the tower to look out in all directions over the park.

In the middle of the nineteenth century, meteorological and astronomical observatories were set up in the Arsenal to gather measurements throughout the park. In 1919, the U.S. Weather Bureau consolidated its equipment and moved to the center of the park, into Belvedere Castle. The weather bureau set up offices, winterized the building, added doors and windows to all the arched masonry openings, and most importantly, removed the tower's conical slate roof to make way for weather-monitoring equipment. The northwest and southwest pavilions eventually deteriorated and were removed by 1930, and soon after, the second-floor terrace was closed off. The most stunning blow to the Belvedere

*C*ompleted in 1872, Belvedere Castle has served in turns as a meteorological and astronomical observatory and as an educational facility for children.

*B*elvedere Castle, designed by Vaux in 1867, was intended to be a romantic architectural novelty on the park's skyline.

occurred in the early 1960s, when the automation of weather equipment left the building vacant of bureau staff, and it was ultimately boarded up. Vandals quickly took control of the structure, hastening its physical decay and hiding the sparkle of the mica schist under a blanket of graffiti.

Plans for restoring the Belvedere began as early as 1973, although work did not begin until 1980. When work was finally under way, new stone was shaped and set where original fragments were missing, including some pieces that were shipped in from New Hampshire, Virginia, and upstate New York. The original terraces and pavilions were rebuilt, the tower was restored to its original conical form, the eroded cast-iron support structure for the stone floor and ceilings was replaced with steel, and the original painting and finishing was, where discernible, restored. The Belvedere reopened in the spring of 1983.

Today, the role that Belvedere Castle plays in the park has grown considerably. Not only is it a destination for 100,000 visitors each year, but it has also become a first-rate education facility for children. With a grant from the federal government and guidance from the Central Park Conservancy and the Parks Department, the castle has been named the Central Park Learning Center and offers courses on park history and environmental science. Throughout the year, instructors and volunteers lead programs for local schools and families that draw upon the natural resources of the park.

THE CAROUSEL

Since the first small, homemade carousel was installed in Central Park in 1871, generations of New York children have made the carousel an essential stop on any visit to the park.

The first carousel to grace the park was turned by two blind animals—a horse and a mule—who trudged around an underground pit and responded to one or two stomps on the floor above them. This archaic approach was replaced around the turn of the century by a steam-driven version, which brought pleasure to tens of thousands of children until fire destroyed it in 1924. A third carousel, with forty-eight small horses standing three abreast, operated on the same site until it, too, burned in 1950.

The present carousel was the result of a passionate search by the Parks Department for an authentic replacement for their beloved attraction. Carousels flourished in the United States between 1880 and 1930, and it was through a stroke of luck, after almost a year of looking, that a vintage carousel was located at the end of the streetcar line in Coney Island in the old BMT trolley terminal. The Board of Transportation, which had no use for such a toy, offered it to the Parks Department for free. The machine had been crafted by Stein and Goldstein of Brooklyn in 1908 when the borough had been the center of the wood-carving community. While a brand-new model might have cost $25,000, including glaring fluorescent lights and a jukebox, the total cost of their rare find was twenty-six hundred dollars, mainly for the materials necessary to dismantle the carousel and transfer it to the repair shop.

The carousel, with its fifty-eight hand-carved horses, is one of the largest in the United States. Each row has four horses, rising in size from the center to the perimeter of the platform, and the largest of these is three-quarters the size of a real horse. In fact, the carousel is so large and so fast that it was never intended to be the kind where children reach for a brass ring. The carving on this carousel is a particularly fine example of folk art, with the most ornate designs relegated to the largest animals.

In 1983, the carousel and its building were restored, and the machinery and the organ completely overhauled. Today, the carousel stands proudly as one facet of the park that faithfully indulges a child's fantasy.

Fifty-eight hand-carved horses, originally crafted in 1908, grace the Central Park carousel.

A closer look (*below, left and right*) reveals the fine detail of the woodwork on the vintage carousel.

*T*he carousel (*above*) has been a popular stop for adults and children alike since the first one was installed in the park in 1871.

The Blockhouse, just inside the park at One Hundred and Tenth Street, was erected around 1814 as a defense against the threat of British invasion.

THE BLOCKHOUSE AND THE FORTS

Standing in the middle of modern-day Central Park as joggers run by in neon spandex tights and children play touch football on the Great Lawn, it is nearly impossible to imagine the historical significance attached to this piece of land. The park, however, has a very rich and varied historical past. During the Revolutionary War and the War of 1812, the hills of Harlem Heights in the northern end of the park served as strategic military outposts for both American and invading British troops. And although very little physical evidence remains to remind us of that history, it is fascinating to visit these places and envision life in colonial Manhattan.

In the days before Manhattan was graded to lay down flat streets, before the trenches were filled and hills were worn down, and before landfills added acres to the width of Manhattan Island, there was a natural battlement that ran from the Hudson River to the Harlem Creek marsh. The only convenient way through this mini–mountain range

was McGowan's Pass, a small gap named for a popular tavern of the time. The current site of McGowan's Pass would be just west of Fifth Avenue at One Hundred and Sixth Street. Twice in American history this little gap played an important role.

In September 1776, after the British defeated the Americans at the Battle of Long Island, the Redcoats headed for McGowan's Pass in an effort to trap General George Washington's troops on the southern end of Manhattan. Washington realized the plan and managed to lead his men through the pass and to the north just in time. A rear guard of American troops delayed the British just long enough to ensure Washington's escape and fled, leaving the pass in the hands of the British. After the Battle of Fort Washington two months later, the victorious British led some 2,800 captured American troops back through the pass and into prisons in British-held Manhattan. For the rest of the Revolutionary War, Manhattan and McGowan's Pass were held by the

British. It was not until seven years later that victorious American troops under the command of General Henry Knox took back the pass and marched through Harlem Heights on their way to liberate the city.

Thirty years later, a new sense of suspicion and dread entered New York. As the War of 1812 unfolded, it seemed that the British might attempt an attack on Manhattan from the north. When the British bombarded Stonington, Connecticut, on August 10, 1814, a call went out among able-bodied men to strengthen the defenses around the city. Immediately, a series of fortifications was built around Harlem Heights. Primary among these was the Blockhouse, a short stone structure that was erected just inside the current boundary of the park at One Hundred and Tenth Street, atop a steep escarpment. The Blockhouse was originally outfitted with a wooden roof and a revolving gun with 360-degree exposure. In addition to the Blockhouse, three other forts were also built or resupplied: Fort Fish, Fort Clinton, and Nutter's Battery. All three of these structures were clustered around the same promontories between One Hundred and Fifth and One Hundred and Seventh Street, completing a more or less equilateral triangle.

*A*n 1814 drawing of the gate at McGowan's Pass (*left*), where American soldiers stood watch over the main entrance to Manhattan island.

A view of Fort Fish and Nutter's Battery in 1814 (*right*).

In fact, the British never did invade Manhattan, and a peace treaty—the Treaty of Ghent—was signed only three months later. Not a single shot was fired at any of the forts, and they were immediately abandoned. Today, the Blockhouse is the oldest remaining building in Central Park, and one of only two currently standing that predate the park itself (the other is the Arsenal at Sixty-fourth Street and Fifth Avenue). Nothing remains of the other forts, although their locations remain well defined and are worth a visit.

Although the peace settlement rendered the forts virtually useless, the present-day existence of the Blockhouse serves a dual purpose: not only does it remind us of the nation's and the region's history, but it also reminds us of the topography of Manhattan before the park was constructed. The fortifications in the northern end of the park were all suitable lookout posts to the surrounding countryside, with a view that reached as far away as Westchester County. The buildings of Harlem have since blocked the horizon, but standing at the fort sites, one can still get a sense of the kind of view they once commanded. What remains of the Blockhouse is a fine vantage point on New York in the eighteenth and nineteenth centuries.

THE DAIRY

The Dairy, the Victorian Gothic building located in the center of Central Park at Sixty-fifth Street, was once the focal point of the section of the park known as the Children's Area. Designed by Olmsted and Vaux as part of their "social plan" for the park, the Dairy was one of several structures, including the Playground, the Carousel, the Kinderburg Shelter, and the Children's Cottage and Cow Stable, that was placed in the southern end of the park to facilitate access from the park's main southern entrances for young people. While the construction of Central Park continued for more than a generation, the Dairy was one of the first amenities of the original Greensward Plan to be completed.

When Olmsted and Vaux decided to put a dairy in Central Park, they were not only pursuing an aesthetic goal established in European romantic landscapes (milkmaids were common sights in private European parks), but they were also seeking to fulfill a far more practical objective: providing fresh milk to New York City. In the nineteenth century, New Yorkers had only two sources for fresh milk—farmers from out of town who brought in their excess production and city brewers who sought an alternate trade by feeding cows with mash left over from the brewing process. Thanks to Olmsted and Vaux's vision, parents and children were sold milk from cows that were pastured right in the park. The cows were stabled in the Children's Cottage (once found southwest of the Dairy) and grazed on the meadow between the Dairy and the northern loop of the pond (now covered by Wollman Rink).

The Dairy building itself was designed by Vaux and erected in 1870. The structure consists of two side-by-side buildings that are similar in form. One is a solid edifice, a building with walls, floors, and ceilings, while the other—a loggia—is a lighter structural imitation, a framed roof of handcrafted wooden beams and open sides. The combination of the two leads to an abundance of diverse romantic imagery. From one angle, the steeple and window treatment are reminiscent of a church; from another, the patterned cutout hand railings and sharp roof look like a mountain chalet. No matter how it appears, the synthesis of these various styles makes the Dairy uniquely representative of nineteenth-century art and culture.

For most of the twentieth century, the Dairy was used only as a storeroom. By the 1950s, the building's loggia, which had been badly damaged by neglect and misuse, was removed completely. In 1979, with $187,000 in private donations, the

building's interior was restored, and it was converted from a storage space back into a public hall. Two years later, the elaborate wooden loggia was rebuilt following the original drawings, and painted Victorian colors. Since its restoration, the Dairy has served as the park's visitor center under the auspices of the Central Park Conservancy, providing a home for educational programs and exhibits as well as the main source of park information for the general public.

*T*he Dairy (*above*), originally designed by Vaux and erected in 1870, was completely renovated in 1979 and now serves as the park's primary visitor center.

*T*he steeple atop the Dairy loggia (*opposite*) is brightly painted following the classic Victorian style.

Chapter Five

A DAY IN THE LIFE OF A CITY TREASURE

From a historical perspective, Central Park acts as a looking glass of the changing values of our culture. In the century and more that the park has been vital to New York City living, we have witnessed the increase of exercise as a form of leisure; the growth of the park as a center for inexpensive cultural pursuits and entertainment on a mass scale; and quite simply, the increased need for the park as a haven from the growing concrete web of Manhattan. The park is a reflection of our own cultural priorities—what we choose to do with our free time—and it has been managed in such a way that allows each of us to express ourselves within its borders.

Central Park is about specialized recreation and unregulated relaxation. Just about every popular sport and game—and a few that are not so popular—has been given special consideration: There are pony tracks, bowling greens, tennis courts, swimming pools, rowboats, skating rinks, and baseball diamonds. Even so, Olmsted's vision of rural scenery for city dwellers has not been eclipsed by the creation of these facilities.

There is perhaps no better way to get a feel for what the park means to New Yorkers than to take a peek at the people who use it on a regular basis, particularly the athletes, artists, and their audiences who flock to the park with a certain homing instinct. What follows is a snapshot of the public at play in New York City's very own backyard.

New Yorkers escape the tumult of the city by spending an afternoon on the Central Park Lake.

RUNNING AND THE RESERVOIR

Because Central Park was created as a public space for the people of New York City, its use reflects the most popular athletic pursuits of the day. Historically, walking has been the favorite park activity, but jogging now challenges its primacy. Runners now cover the entire expanse of the park and come from every walk of life and every age group.

Many joggers find that running in the park keeps them emotionally as well as physically fit. With the hectic hustle and bustle of life in the city, running can be as therapeutic as it is healthful. To many who have moved to New York from greener pastures, running in the park can also be an important connection to their suburban or rural past.

The hub of running in the park is undoubtedly the jogging track surrounding the reservoir. Since 1862, when the new reservoir was built, the track around the perimeter has acted as a pedestrian walkway. In 1982, given the rise in jogging's popularity, the pedestrian dirt path was resurfaced with a mix of sand, cinder, and clay to make the area better suited for the huge influx of joggers. The track has become such a popular destination for competitive and recreational joggers alike that the park entrance at East Ninetieth Street has been nicknamed the "runner's gate."

The abundance of runners in the park not only makes for a supportive athletic community, but provides a wealth of competitive opportunities as well. At the center of this competition is the New York Road Runners Club. Founded in 1958 with forty-two members, the NYRRC now boasts 29,000 members nationally; its headquarters is a half block from the park on East Eighty-ninth Street. The NYRRC sponsors more than 150 races each year in the park, including a competitive series held every Sunday throughout the year. This sort of park use requires close cooperation from the Parks Department, which issues a permit to the club for each organized activity. In return, the club sponsors a safety patrol consisting of volunteers who monitor the primary running routes and maintain constant contact with the local police precinct.

In addition to the weekly competitions, the NYRRC helps to coordinate some of the major athletic events in the city, including the Fifth Avenue Mile, the New York Games, and the grandfather of them all, the New York Marathon. With 25,000 runners from eighty countries around the world participating, the marathon weaves its way through all five New York boroughs before a triumphal entry into the park at the southwest corner and a climactic finish in front of Tavern on the Green.

Running and the park have a particularly special kinship, because running is one of the few activities that does not disturb the tender balance of nature that exists in the park. Mayor Lindsay first closed the park to cars during the weekend so that joggers (as well as walkers and bikers) can enjoy their exercise and meditation undisturbed by the normal flow of traffic.

© New York City Parks Photo Archive

*T*he running track (*left*) that circles the reservoir is the unofficial hub of competitive and recreational jogging in New York City.

*T*he reservoir (*opposite and right*) predates Olmsted and Vaux's design and followed the plan of Egbert Viele, the chief engineer of Central Park when Olmsted became its superintendent.

Skating was one of the first athletic pursuits to be enjoyed regularly in Central Park.

SKATING AND SOCIAL HISTORY

The winter season in New York has always had great appeal to city folk and out-of-towners alike, and Central Park by its very nature has been an attractive destination during the wintertime for more than a century. In December 1858, Central Park was the scene for a new chapter in city history and, it could be argued, an advancement toward women's equality. With the onset of winter and the completion of a part of the Lake, New Yorkers began their first season of ice skating.

The movements of a throng of skaters, on a clear day, chasing each other in gleeful mood over the crystal ceiling of the imprisoned lake, the fur clad inmates of a thousand gay vehicles coursing along the silver snow to the music of the bells, the dusky foliage of the fir and pine on the adjacent heights, wrapped with wreaths of fleecy white; leafless branches strung with a fairy network of icy pearls, frail but gorgeous as it glistens

and flashes with a thousand hues in every glance of the sunlight, form in our midst a winter scene unmatched by that of any capital or country of modern times, because it is obtainable only in a climate, amid an extent of population of wealth and liberality, such as peculiarly characterizes this Queen City of the Western Hemisphere.

—Report of the Central Park Commissioners, 1863

This was not simply the advent of an athletic pastime, but the dawn of a social revolution; ice skating became the first form of exercise made available to women (outside of horseback riding, which was reserved for the wealthy). The first skating pond was in the middle of the park at Seventy-second Street, and as men and women began mingling freely on the ice, the popularity of the sport soared even further. Initially, it was very difficult for New Yorkers to find the proper equipment for their new hobby, but by the second year, more than sixty thousand pairs of skates were sold, many of those to women who were exercising regularly for the first time.

Up until then, the premiere winter sport had been sleighing. Grand coaches with plumes and bells, driven by aristocratic owners, would take to the park drives as soon as the first snow began to stick. With the advent of skating, entirely new opportunities opened up for New Yorkers who were not as well-heeled.

The popularity of skating rose to a feverish pitch throughout the city in the last quarter of the nineteenth century. In order to report the skating conditions in the park without the use of such modern-day devices as televisions, telephones, or radios, a white flag with a red ball was hoisted over the Arsenal and Belvedere Castle when the ice was safe. Commuters were so caught up in the sport that streetcars on the park routes would fly miniature pennants when conditions were favorable. On the periphery of the park, elite operations such as the Manhattan Athletic Club sprang up to cater to the skating tastes of the upper reaches of New York society, charging a quarter and up for admission.

Skating practically revolutionized the use of the park itself. Since daily attendance on the frozen ponds and lakes occasionally reached one hundred thousand, the sport attracted the additional services of vendors to the park. With so many people participating in this phenomenon, it is no wonder that skating was extremely popular for spectators as well.

*U*ntil the advent of skating, sleighing was the premiere winter sport in the park, a pastime affordable only to the very wealthy. Here, winter sleigh rides at the turn of the century keep the snow-covered park drives bustling with traffic.

The hill facing the lake was black with spectators, the spacious hollow where the lake should have been was one solid mass of human beings, their faces glinting as they darted hither and thither, in and out, like the changing reflection of sunlight on the dancing ripples of a broad, windswept sheet of water. The ladies, arrayed in gay plaid costumes without furs, joined in the spirit with a zest and activity that made heavy wraps undesirable. Fancy skaters were out in uncommonly large numbers.
—New York Times, 1880

All across the country, the booming popularity of ice skating owed a debt, in part, to the opening of the lakes in Central Park.

Despite the increasing interest and the rise in participation, there was still one factor that managed to dampen the popular enthusiasm for skating in the park: the unreliable New York weather. During any given year, the throngs of skaters who flocked to the park were at the mercy of the elements, hoping that the winter would stay cold enough long enough to keep the ice solidly frozen. Many seasons, the unreliable weather

made night skating the preferred activity—the lower evening temperatures ensured an icy smooth surface on the lakes. But it was not until 1950, with the construction of Wollman Rink, that skating was really possible throughout the entire winter. Rather than seeking out the frozen inlets and coves surrounding the sometimes-frozen lakes, skaters could now depend on a convenient if less romantic alternative.

The development and maintenance of Wollman Rink has not been without its share of problems. The task of freezing and maintaining refrigeration on an open-air rink in a climate such as New York's is huge, as is the task of maintaining a recreation center of such enormous demand. In 1966, the park attempted to divert some of the skating crowds by the construction of Lasker Rink where the Loch empties into the Harlem Meer near the park's northern border. Lasker seemed to suffer from the same fear of safety in the park that Wollman had experienced at its opening. Back at Wollman, with attendance dropping from nearly a half million in the 1950s and early 1960s to a trickle of less than 100,000 in the entire 1979 season, the Parks Department realized that major renovation was necessary. Unfortunately, the funding for these works was as scarce as the crowds. After six years of starting and stopping construction and a protracted game of political football, the "new" rink was finally completed in 1986 under the watchful eye of developer Donald Trump. With wintertime skating every day of the week, the rink as it stands today is once again a popular attraction for those seeking cold-weather recreation.

©Allan Detrick

*W*inter walks in Central Park (*left*) have always been a popular pursuit for hearty souls seeking a quieter, sleepier park.

© Sara Cedar Miller/Central Park Conservancy

*T*he construction of Wollman Rink (*above, left*) in 1950 provided park visitors with a convenient place to skate all winter long. New Yorkers young and old (*above, right*) have been learning how to skate in Central Park for almost 150 years.

*R*ollerbladers test their skills against the slalom course set up on "the Hill" to the west of Sheep Meadow.

ROLLERBLADING INTO THE FUTURE

The park has witnessed—and sometimes even catalyzed—some of the most popular cultural fads of the last three decades: Hula-Hoops, sit-ins, streaking, skateboards. A few skeptical critics might place Rollerblading in this group of short-term fads doomed to obscurity, but judging by its overwhelming popularity and recent entrenchment in the park, others would tell you that it's here to stay.

Rollerblading, or in-line skating, started becoming popular in the park around 1987. Conventional roller-skating had been an established form of recreation in the park for years, whether skaters chose to join in the ring of freestyle dancers just to the east of Sheep Meadow or to test themselves on a makeshift slalom course established on "the Hill" to the west of Sheep Meadow. But linking roller-skating with Rollerblading is like associating cross-country with downhill skiing.

While roller skaters lean toward freestyle movement and artistic self-expression on skates, Rollerbladers are generally out for speed and exercise.

Rollerblading originated on the long paved walkways of Venice Beach, California. Given the speedy cross-country travel of social trends, it did not take long to make its way to New York. With the establishment of a few retail outlets and the increased availability of "'blades," popularity in the park was not far behind. In 1988, the Big Apple RoadSkaters Association (BARA) was founded as a way to promote a skating community and a venue for informal competition. In 1991, BARA sponsored the first Rollerblading marathon in New York, and new competitive events are planned regularly. On a more casual basis, in-line skaters have become almost as commonplace in the park as runners, lapping the perimeter drives with strength and grace on evenings and weekends. BARA sponsors a regular clinic on skating technique every Thursday and promotes a family "park skate" on Sunday afternoons, but perhaps the most popular event from an audience standpoint is the weekly slalom course and clinic. The new course, with two levels of difficulty, is in the same location as the original course on "the Hill" and attracts skaters of all shapes and sizes who go gliding down a lane of orange cones in a test of gravity-defying dexterity. Still, the real winners are the gallery of onlookers who cheer on the top daredevil performances.

BARA works closely with the Parks Department to ensure the safety of skaters and pedestrians alike. "The Hill" has become an unofficial meeting center for bladers thanks to the Parks Department, and in return, BARA has made strides toward developing a skate patrol to monitor primary skate routes as a security measure in conjunction with the Central Park precinct.

CROQUET AND LAWN BOWLING

There are few Manhattan scenes more out of place yet more memorable than men and women lawn bowling and playing croquet in the heart of Central Park. Outfitted in white uniforms and concentrating intensely on small colored balls as they roll across the manicured green lawn, these players seem more reminiscent of Victorian England than representative of modern New York. Still, the scene is real, taking place at the Central Park Lawn Sports Center, located just north of Sheep Meadow near West Sixty-ninth Street. The Lawn Sports Center consists of two square playing greens and a nearby "clubhouse" used for equipment storage. While these green courts are officially maintained by the park, they are actually the domain of the New York Lawn Bowling Club and the New York Croquet Club, two independent organizations. The Lawn Bowling Club was organized in Central Park in 1926, but traces its roots to the colonization of Manhattan, while the Croquet Club, founded in 1966, is a product of more modern history. Despite the differences in their

*T*he New York Lawn Bowling Club has been enjoying the use of Central Park since 1926.

histories, the two clubs coexist fairly peacefully on the greens that have been in place in the park for almost seventy years.

One simply has to take a brief tour downtown to see the impact that lawn bowling has had on New Yorkers. Bowling Green Park was established at the southern tip of Manhattan in 1733 as the first official site for the sport in the New World. The greens in Central Park were established 193 years later and the New York Lawn Bowling Club has been at the center of the action ever since.

Arguably the oldest recreational organization to be affiliated with the park, the New York Lawn Bowling Club counts Peter Minuit, the Dutch colonial administrator who bought Manhattan Island from the Indians in 1626, among its founding members. Because of its English roots, the sport went through a period of low popularity around the time of the Revolutionary War but was revived in the early 1900s by three men—George Reid, William Crawford, and Tom Lennox—who managed to establish the sport as a regular activity in Central Park. In 1926, the first of two greens was built in the park, once again with the support of the Dutch government, which donated 1,500 bulbs to the park for planting around the perimeter of the green. Four years later, the second green was completed.

The current members of the Lawn Bowling Club consider themselves to be environmental conservators almost as much as competitors. They take pride in the fact that the proper maintenance of a professional-quality bowling green requires almost as much of their energy as the game itself. From varying the direction of their field of play (east-west one month, north-south the next) to overseeing the trimming and irrigation of the lawn and the planting of the boundaries, all the members are involved in the conservation and maintenance of the lawn. As one of 150 community-sponsored greens around the country, the New York players are prepared for the scrutiny of their fellow bowlers from around the states.

The New York club boasts approximately 135 members, ranging in age from teenagers to senior citizens. From May through November, card-carrying members are welcome on the greens every day but Monday for informal competition. On Tuesdays, Thursdays, and weekends, official club games are held at 1:00 P.M. to sharpen skills and heighten the competitive atmosphere among members. Roughly fifteen tournaments per year round out the club's schedule of seasonal events.

The New York Croquet Club, despite its members' formal appearance in competition attire, is actually a more casual organization than the Lawn Bowling Club, dedicated simply to the enjoyment and proliferation of the game of croquet. The club, which was founded in 1966, encourages croquet at all levels of play, from free Tuesday-night clinics to weekend tournaments that take place in the summer. As a member of the United States Croquet Association, the NYCC sends

its best players to national and international tournaments throughout the year, although Central Park remains the home turf to the 150 New York club members. In addition to supporting maintenance of the park, the club also supplies croquet equipment to its members, for whom the $1,500 price tag for a set of croquet clubs and wickets would otherwise be prohibitive.

The limited space available to the lawn bowlers and the croquet players means that they have to share. While the presence of two greens enabled the lawn bowlers to use them in rotation for many years, preserving one while using the other, the limited space now means that the two groups trade off greens every month, and that both greens are used constantly. This is hardly an ideal situation, but it forces both groups to be extra diligent in their maintenance and preservation methods. Ultimately, it is the responsibility of the Parks Department to seed and mow the greens, but they rely on the individual organizations to be self-sufficient on a daily and even weekly basis.

Both clubs have a symbiotic relationship with the park: the Parks Department issues a seasonal permit to the Lawn Bowling Club and the Croquet Club for use of the Lawn Sports Center from May through November, and the clubs in turn contribute financially to the maintenance and preservation of the area.

*M*embers of the New York
Croquet Club are not required to wear "competition whites" in
order to play but do so out of a dedication to the spirit of the sport.

*S*ome early views of Conservatory Water (*above and opposite*) before the construction of the Kerbs Boathouse.

MODEL-YACHT RACING AND THE CONSERVATORY WATER

There is a unique spot in Central Park where New Yorkers flock to watch other New Yorkers at play, where the spectating is almost as glorious as the participating: the Conservatory Water on East Seventy-third Street, home of the Central Park Model Yacht Club (CPMYC).

On Saturdays during the warm-weather months, the blue surface of Conservatory Water is alive with small white sails, its perimeter dotted alternately with skippers operating remote-control boats and wide-eyed spectators. This is the home of turn-of-the-century model schooners handcrafted from teak, sailing side-by-side with streamlined models made of fiberglass and Kevlar that boast the cutting edge of nautical technology. A glance around the faces of the boat owners—particularly at race time—will tell you that this is more than a whimsical childhood fantasy being acted out. At upwards of $700 per boat (with some costing more than $2,000), these models represent an investment of both time and money, and the owners will be the first to say that the dividend they get in return is sheer joy.

The motivating force behind these landlocked sailors, the Central Park Model Yacht Club, is one of the older organizations to use the park on a regular basis. Dating back to 1916, the club can trace its origins to a handful of men who sailed their boats in the Belvedere Reservoir (the "old" reservoir) just after the Civil War. Formally attired for their nautical pursuits in straw boaters and white trousers, these original sportsmen did not have the benefits of remote-controls as they launched their boats from shore. Using first a fixed sail and later a wind-vane device attached to the rudder, the boat owners had to wait until their models made their own way back to shore to retrieve them. Needless to say, the advancements of modern technology have made the sport more convenient as well as more exciting.

Model sailing in Central Park has been interrupted only twice since its inception. During World War I, the city closed the reservoir for all but the most essential use, forcing the club to move south to its current home at Conservatory Water. The second interruption, when Conservatory Water was drained to conserve water throughout World War II, left the skippers high and dry.

The development and advancement of the CPMYC received an essential boost from the construction of the Kerbs Memorial Boathouse in 1954. When the club had first moved to Conservatory Water, the only existing structure was an old wooden building that neither preserved the model boats nor did justice to the beautiful landscape of the park. Jeanne E. Kerbs donated the Boathouse to the city in memory of her parents, who had lived at Fifth Avenue and Seventy-fourth Street and watched the sailing from their

The Sail Boat Pond, Central Park, New York City.

home. The donation also included an endowment for the upkeep and maintenance of the Boathouse and for an annual children's sailing competition.

Model-yacht racing today remains a wonderfully popular event. Conservatory Water, built thirty feet (9.1 m) below street level and hidden from a steady breeze by trees and tall buildings, is hardly ideal for sailors, but perfect for 360 degrees of spectating. Today's elaborate, high-tech miniature sailboats owe a debt to the pilotless drone airplanes of World War II for the advent of radio control. By the mid-seventies, the circuitry of remote controls became small enough for racing boats, and several hobby manufacturers helped to promote and develop the sport. While the Model Yacht Racing Association of America (formed back in 1922) was cynical about the use of these navigational systems, the formation of the American Model Yacht Association helped to establish these units as the standard of international competition.

The technological advances that have gone hand in hand with model-yacht racing have priced the sport out of the reach of children, but at the same time have helped it gain the attention of big boat sailors, who look upon these lilliputian craft as a test ground for new aerodynamic and hydraulic advances.

Conservatory Water and the Kerbs Boathouse are not, in fact, the exclusive domain of the Central Park Model Yacht

*M*odel-boat races on the
Conservatory Water are a weekly event that regularly attract
hundreds of spectators.

Club. Anyone with a model sailboat (including any child with a small motorboat) is allowed on the pond, and anyone with a park permit may store a model in the Boathouse, regardless of club membership. The club does reserve from 10:00 A.M. to 2:00 P.M. on Saturdays from March through November for their racing series.

The relationship between the yacht club and the Parks Department is one of mutual admiration and respect. While the maintenance of Conservatory Water is officially the responsibility of the park, the officers and members of the CPMYC take it upon themselves to maintain the area around the pond, remove leaves and branches from the water, and keep the Boathouse clean for visitors (it is open to the public on weekends). The Parks Department, in return, cooperates with the yacht club in the storage and security of their model boats, in the annual maintenance of the Boathouse structure, and in providing support when the CPMYC identifies problems in their small sector of the park.

The striking visual image of colorful model sailboats streaking across the surface of Conservatory Water is one of the most memorable in the park, if not the entire city. As perhaps the preeminent model-boating site in the country, Conservatory Water and the CPMYC look forward to a successful future of dazzling New York residents and visitors alike.

*A*dvancements in the design of model sailboats have made Conservatory Water a testing ground for nautical technology as much as a playground for zealous sailors.

*T*he statue of
Hans Christian Andersen on the
west side of Conservatory Water
is a focal point for children's
activities in the park.

STORYTELLING FOR EVERYONE

The greatest strength of Central Park is its ability to be so many different things to different people. In the last fifty years or so, a particular effort has been made in the park to introduce events and activities for children and families as well as adults. The Cottage Marionette Theater is one example of this effort. On a more informal basis, storytelling for children in Central Park has become another successful—and important—example.

In 1956, in memory of the one hundred and fiftieth anniversary of Hans Christian Andersen's birth, the Danish-American Women's Association sponsored the construction of a statue to honor the famous Danish author of children's literature. The statue, located on the west side of Conservatory Water at Seventy-third Street, quickly became the focal point for children's activities in the park. Within a year of the statue's dedication, a society was founded to carry on the storytelling tradition of Hans Christian Andersen.

For thirty-four years, the Hans Christian Andersen Society has provided readings in the park for children. From June through September, between fifty and two hundred children and parents gather at the statue every Saturday at 11:00 A.M. to hear children's stories. Every other week, the stories are exclusively Hans Christian Andersen's, but the society also presents works from other prominent and popular children's authors.

The HCA Society is not alone. The New York Public Library also sponsors storytelling for children in conjunction with the Parks Department. So as not to compete for their audience, the library chooses Wednesdays in the summer for their readings.

With this abundance of public storytelling and its sustained popularity over the years, there is little surprise that the audiences have gradually become more and more mature, as adult New Yorkers realize that youth is not a requirement for enjoying a leisurely summer morning with a good story.

PUPPETS AND THE COTTAGE MARIONETTE THEATER

In addition to the Children's Zoo and organized storytelling in the park, the marionette and puppet shows at the Swedish Cottage represent Central Park's active efforts to provide diverse and enriching entertainment for children. Because these shows are often a child's first exposure to live theater, the puppeteers strive to expose young New Yorkers to the energy and variety of theatrical experience.

The Swedish Cottage, located on the west side of the park at Seventy-ninth Street, was originally called the Swedish Schoolhouse and was designed for the 1876 Centennial Exposition in Philadelphia. The building was constructed as an example of Swedish building style and design and was erected in Sweden before being transported to Philadelphia for assembly. At the end of the fair, the New York City Department of Parks decided to purchase the schoolhouse for $1,500, and after a year of planning, it was moved to its

The statue of Alice in Wonderland, at the northern end of Conservatory Water, has been a favorite climbing spot for generations of New York City children.

*S*treet performers are just one of the many diversions that enchant children on a sunny day in Central Park.

present site in Central Park. Initially used as a toolhouse and storage facility, the schoolhouse was converted to a women's comfort station and lunchroom in 1900. Following protests by Swedish organizations, the building was remodeled for more "appropriate" use as a park laboratory in 1912. During World War II, the schoolhouse served as district headquarters of civil defense, and it was only after the end of the war that the schoolhouse was turned back to the Parks Department, which designated its use to the Cottage Marionette Theater for its workshop and headquarters.

The Cottage Marionette Theater was founded in 1939 by parks commissioner Robert Moses. The original company, devoted exclusively to marionette performances for children, toured schools in the winter and parks and playgrounds in the summer. In 1947, the company moved into its current home in the Swedish Cottage. The troupe continued their touring until 1971, when a new marionette truck that opened to become a portable stage and four similar trucks for hand puppets extended the program beyond the park walls and into the streets. It wasn't until 1973 that the Swedish Cottage itself was redesigned to accommodate a small theater, giving audiences a central location to see productions.

In 1980, with the benefit of a large full-time staff and sizable public interest and support, a group of the marionette company branched off to form a hand-puppet troupe. Housed in the small brick building adjacent to the Heckscher Playground fields, the Heckscher Puppet House played host to school groups and audiences of children several times a week. Unfortunately, with the city and the Parks Department facing fiscal limitations, the program was discontinued in 1991.

At the Cottage Marionette Theater, marionette shows continue to play nine months of the year. From November through May, performances such as *Jack and the Beanstalk* and *The Magic Flute* are held during the week for school groups and on weekends for the general public. During July and August, the theater performs for summer camps. All of the shows are created by the puppeteers, who are artists in their own right from several different fields. They not only perform but also write the plays, construct and costume the puppets, and design all aspects of the production.

SHAKESPEARE, SYMPHONIES, AND PUBLIC ENTERTAINMENT

Beginning with the first park concert in 1859, music has played an important role in the life of Central Park. For Olmsted and Vaux, recreation did not mean athletic pursuit as much as it meant stimulation for the heart and soul. This thinking was clearly reflected in the park design, with its numerous opportunities for personal reflection and cultural enrichment.

The Mall, already the main social center of the park in the nineteenth century, also became the focal point for music. A floating bandstand had been designed for use in the nearby Lake, but Olmsted and Vaux declined to use it because they felt that the area to the west of the Mall was the best site for public performances: It provided easy access from the major thoroughfares, commanded an attractive view, and was altogether "conspicuous without being obtrusive." Despite some failed attempts, the closest anyone came to an aquatic performance was a ten-man cornet band that occasionally performed from a boat, serenading audiences on shore.

In 1862, a small but ornately decorated iron bandstand, which was open on all sides, was constructed for the west side of the Mall to act as a music pavilion. When it was finished, audiences on foot and in passing carriages would gather under the pergola, a rustic open-air shelter that stood atop the hill overlooking the Mall, to listen to the music emanating from the bandstand. At times, these bandstand concerts were so popular that the neighborhood railway companies had to run extra cars to accommodate the increased number of people coming up from downtown. In general, however, the music of the day encouraged appreciation but little participation.

Saturday concerts on the Mall, this one (*above*) in 1863, could attract as many as forty thousand people to the area on a single day.

An 1870 photo (*left*) shows the elaborate drinking fountains once found on the Mall.

© New York City Parks Photo Archive

𝒯he Barbra Streisand concert on the Great Lawn in 1967 was the largest gathering to date in the park's history.

In 1921, with the rise of the band concert movement in the United States, a retired merchant and banker named Elkan Naumburg offered the city $100,000 to build an elaborate bandshell. Built across the Mall from the old one, the new structure was not open on all sides, and in order to avoid interference with the flow of traffic in the Mall, the structure was eventually backed into the existing pergola. Much was made about the fact that this would deny a view of the performance to the casual passersby in their carriages. Nonetheless, the rise in popular music prompted an increase in musical events, and soon after the new bandshell opened in 1923, it was attracting audiences of up to 30,000 people five times a week.

Throughout the life of the Naumburg Bandshell, the space has been used for everything from jazz, rock, classical, and folk music performances to classically staged opera and theater, with each performance attracting an enthusiastic New York audience devoted to the principle—and the practicality—of free public entertainment.

The power and popularity of mass gatherings in the park saw its heyday in the sixties. With the advent of love-ins, sit-ins, and be-ins, the wide open spaces of Central Park offered something not to be found elsewhere in New York. Still, the sense of bonding and peaceful coexistence that identified a generation also prompted smart businessmen to take advantage of a lucrative situation. Ron Delsener, a producer of rock tours and musical shows, turned the otherwise vacant Wollman Rink into a site for a low-priced rock concert series that began in the summer of 1964. And while this sort of event and others like it brought frequent entertainment to the park, it was performers such as Barbra Streisand who began to draw truly massive crowds. Her concert in the park in 1967 was the largest gathering in the park's history and set a precedent for such performers as Elton John, Diana Ross, and Paul Simon, who each attracted up to 750,000 people.

While the political and artistic climate of the time was conducive to large-scale rallies and loud concerts, the Parks

Department and the New York arts community also provided three opportunities for more classical entertainment. The first two were the summer concert series by the Metropolitan Opera and the New York Philharmonic. Started in 1961 and 1965, respectively, these series of classical events now take place on the Great Lawn (and before its restoration, on Sheep Meadow). The Met and the Philharmonic—two of the major musical powerhouses in the world—joined forces with the Parks Department and corporate sponsors like Mobil Oil and Chemical Bank to provide free performances throughout the summer. As the program expanded, both organizations arranged for touring companies to travel throughout the five boroughs and perform two or three different shows over the course of the summer. The result is that five or six times every summer, Central Park plays host to an audience of more than 100,000 classical music fans who pack a picnic dinner, spread out their checkered tablecloths and blankets, and enjoy a peaceful evening appreciating fine music.

The Metropolitan Opera and the New York Philharmonic perform on a huge mobile stage (*above*) that is erected on the Great Lawn and is dismantled after every performance.

The free concerts in the park provide New Yorkers (*left*) with the opportunity to enjoy a picnic under a starry sky right in the heart of Manhattan.

𝒯he New York Summer Shakespeare Festival playing to a free audience in the Delacorte Theater.

The third opportunity for classical entertainment is the New York Shakespeare Festival, which first appeared in the park in the late fifties. New Yorkers experienced the Shakespeare Workshop, as it was called, under the direction of Joseph Papp when it began in a church basement on the Lower East Side in 1954. Two years later, the Free Shakespeare Summer Festival began at the East River amphitheater. The festival became a permanent part of the Central Park landscape soon afterward, when the portable stage that had toured city parks with the performing troupe collapsed near Belvedere Lake. Through the generosity of George Delacorte, a publishing magnate, the Delacorte Theatre opened on the site in 1962. Each summer since that time, the festival has presented productions of Shakespeare's classics to enthusiastic New York audiences, who often stand in line for six hours or more to get free tickets to each performance. Nearly 100,000 people, New Yorkers and tourists alike, attend free of charge annually.

Aside from the larger and more publicized events, Central Park also runs a busy schedule of smaller cultural events every year, highlighted by the Conservancy's SummerStage Festival, a series of music, dance, and literary performances that explores different cultures as well as traditions. Events run the spectrum from Earth Day celebrations to an "elephant walk" with the pachyderm stars of the Ringling Brothers and Barnum & Bailey Circus.

From the beginning, Central Park has been a resource for the bodies and spirits of New Yorkers from all walks of life, and these city dwellers, in turn, are proud of their oasis in the middle of a concrete desert. Just watch them as they near the vicinity of the park, slow down their race against the clock, and stop to soak in the green beauty.

*A*n enthusiastic SummerStage audience (*above*) on a warm summer day in the park.

*J*ust another day in the park: a parade of elephants (*left*) provided by the Ringling Brothers and Barnum & Bailey Circus.

FOR FURTHER READING

Barlow, Elizabeth. *The Central Park Book*. New York: Central Park Task Force, 1979.

Barlow, Elizabeth. *Frederick Law Olmsted's New York*. New York: Whitney Museum, Frederick A. Praeger, 1972.

Barlow, Elizabeth, et al. *Rebuilding Central Park*. Cambridge, Massachusetts: The MIT Press, 1987.

Caro, Robert. *The Power Broker*. New York: Random House, 1975.

Central Park Association. *The Central Park*. New York: Thomas Seltzer, 1926.

Chadwick, George F. *The Park and the Town: Public Landscape in the 19th and 20th Centuries*. New York: Frederick A. Praeger, 1966.

Cook, Clarence Chatham. *A Description of the New York Central Park*. New York: F. J. Huntington and Co., 1869.

Dutton, Ralph. *The English Garden*. London: B. T. Batsford LTD, 1937.

Fein, Albert. *Frederick Law Olmsted and the American Environment Tradition*. New York: George Braziller, 1972.

Heckscher, August. *Alive in the City*. New York: Scribner and Sons, 1974.

Kinkead, Eugene. *Central Park, 1857–1995*. New York: W. W. Norton & Company, 1990.

McLaughlin, Charles Capen, and Charles Beveridge. *The Papers of Frederick Law Olmsted*. Baltimore: Johns Hopkins University Press, 1983.

Olmsted, Frederick Law, Sr. *Forty Years of Landscape Architecture: Central Park*. Eds. Frederick Law Olmsted, Jr., and Theodora Kimball. Cambridge, Mass.: The MIT Press, 1973.

Parsons, Mabel, ed. *Samuel Parsons and the Central Park of New York*. New York: G. P. Putnam's Sons, 1926.

Reed, Henry Hope, and Sophia Duckworth. *Central Park, A History and Guide*. New York: Clarkson N. Potter, Inc., 1972.

Roper, Laura Wood. *A Biography of Frederick Law Olmsted*. Baltimore: The Johns Hopkins University Press, 1973.

Second Annual Report of the Board of Commissioners of the Department of Public Parks, New York. New York: William C. Bryant & Co., 1872.

INDEX